Meaning and Partiality

Studies in Logic, Language and Information

The *Studies in Logic, Language and Information* book series is the official book series of the European Association for Logic, Language and Information (FoLLI).

The scope of the book series is the logical and computational foundations of natural, formal, and programming languages, as well as the different forms of human and mechanized inference and information processing. It covers the logical, linguistic, psychological and information-theoretic parts of the cognitive sciences as well as mathematical tools for them. The emphasis is on the theoretical and interdisciplinary aspects of these areas.

The series aims at the rapid dissemination of research monographs, lecture notes and edited volumes at an affordable price.

Managing editor: Robin Cooper, University of Edinburgh

Executive editor: Maarten de Rijke, CWI, Amsterdam

Editorial board:

Peter Aczel, Manchester University

Nicholas Asher, The University of Austin, Texas

Jon Barwise, Indiana University, Bloominton

John Etchemendy, CSLI, Stanford University

Dov Gabbay, Imperial College, London

Hans Kamp, Universität Stuttgart

Godehard Link, Universität München

Fernando Pereira, AT&T Bell Laboratories, Murray Hill

Dag Westerståhl, Stockholm University

Meaning and Partiality

Reinhard Muskens

CSLI Publications
Center for the Study of Language and Information
Stanford, California
   &
FoLLI
The European Association for
Logic, Language and Information

Copyright ©1995
Center for the Study of Language and Information
Leland Stanford Junior University
Printed in the United States
99 98 97 96 95   5 4 3 2 1

Library of Congress Cataloging-in-Publication Data

Muskens, Reinhard, 1953–
    Meaning and partiality / Reinhard Muskens
        p. cm. — (Studies in logic, language, and information)
    Includes bibliographical references (p. 133) and indexes.

    ISBN 1-881526-80-1 (cloth)
    ISBN 1-881526-79-8 (paper)

    1. Semantics. 2. Language and logic. I. Title. II. Series.
P325.M84 1995
401'.43—dc20   95-34688
                                                CIP

∞ The acid-free paper used in this book meets the minimum requirements
of the American National Standard for Information Sciences—Permanence of
Paper for Printed Library Materials, ANSI Z39.48-1984.

voor Noor

Contents

Preface

In this book Montague Semantics is partialized by replacing the logic which underlies that system by a partial variant. The result is a theory not unlike Barwise and Perry's original formulation of Situation Semantics or Kratzer's present version of that theory: possible worlds become partial possible worlds or *situations*, ordered by a *part-of* relation. As soon as this natural structure of situations is available within Montague Semantics, the framework supports many analyses of semantic phenomena that were originally carried out within the competing Situation Semantics approach and we thus obtain a synthesis between two semantic frameworks that are usually thought to be incompatible.

As a preliminary step towards partializing Montague Semantics I radically simplify it, taking care that the old theory and its simplification agree in their predictions about ordinary language entailment. The standard formulation of Montague's system is unnecessarily complex: a quagmire of boxes, cups, caps, temporal operators, special notational conventions and special rules constraining the applicability of lambda conversion and universal instantiation, in which the unprepared may well find himself lost. Such complexities do not only obscure the fundamental elegance of the approach and do not only make it difficult to work with, they also make it the case that the theory is hard to generalize and that incorporation of genuinely new ideas is virtually impossible as a consequence. Streamlining the theory is a necessity rather than a luxury given our purposes.

The book originated as my 1989 dissertation, but apart from minor reorganizations and corrections of occasional mistakes I have not revised its contents. The need for an integration of existing semantic frameworks has hardly diminished since 1989 and I flatter myself with the thought that the ideas explained here contribute to a general method for obtaining workable syntheses of various semantic approaches. I have resisted the temptation to include some of my more recent work on combining Montague Semantics and Discourse Representations (see e.g. Muskens 1991a, 1995a,

1995b), although that work certainly has close connections to the ideas presented here and although its methods and general philosophy have much in common with the general approach that is taken presently.

I would like to thank Johan van Benthem and Dick de Jongh for their encouragement and for the attention they generously gave to my work when I was writing this book. They were both wonderful. I also want to thank Henk Barendrecht, Renate Bartsch, Peter van Emde Boas, Paul Dekker, Jan van Eijck, Fritz Hamm, Herman Hendriks, Theo Janssen, Michael Kohlhase, Emiel Krahmer, Manfred Kupfer, Serge Lapierre, Francois Lepage, Noor van Leusen, Michael Morreau, Peter Ruhrberg, Martin Stokhof, Göran Sundholm, Elias Thijsse, Frank Veltman and an anonymous referee for comments and criticisms. Maarten de Rijke volunteered typesetting the manuscript and was the most patient of editors. Most of the research for this book was carried out while I was working for NWO, the Netherlands Organization for Pure and Applied Research, whose support I gratefully acknowledge.

1

Introduction

No formal system can be a satisfactory vehicle for natural language interpretation unless it allows for some degree of underdefinedness. We are finite beings, our capacities for perceiving our surroundings are limited and since the world of phenomena is immensely large this means we can perceive only part of the world. We see, feel and hear parts of reality, not the whole of it, and it seems that a sentence containing a verb of perception like 'John sees a house burn' is most naturally treated as saying that the subject sees an incomplete world in which the embedded sentence is true (see Barwise 1981 for this analysis). But if we want to analyse perception verbs thus, we must introduce some form of incompleteness into our formal system, the system must be able to deal with partial worlds.

This is one reason for 'going partial'; a second (but related) reason is the coarse-grainedness of traditional theories of meaning. Theories based on standard logic conflate meanings of sentences that are classically equivalent, even if these sentences are not strictly synonymous. Here is an example.

(1)   John walks

(2)   John walks and Bill talks or does not talk

According to our intuitions these are not synonymous sentences in the strictest sense, the first one does not even mention Bill or his talking, while the second one does. But no theory based on classical logic will be able to discriminate between the two. In Montague Grammar, for example, the meaning of (1) will be a certain set of possible worlds (the set of worlds in which John walks) and the meaning of (2) will be the intersection of this set with the set that is the meaning of 'Bill talks or does not talk'. But the latter sentence is a classical tautology and so its meaning will be the set of *all* possible worlds. Hence (1) and (2) are predicted to be synonymous, which strictly speaking they are not.

At first blush it might seem that this incongruence between theoretical prediction and observed fact is not that important. The theory, after all, gives a correct prediction about the relation of *entailment* here, even if

1

it does not predict our intuitions about strict synonymy accurately. The two sentences entail each other, if one is true the other is, and this fact correctly follows from Montague's theory. We see here that the relation of strict synonymy is somewhat more fine-grained (or somewhat stronger) than the relation of co-entailment is. Cannot we take the position that, although this is true, the latter relation is a good enough approximation of the former and that the classical theory, since it gets the facts about entailment right, will suffice as an approximation to the theory of synonymy in natural language?

Unfortunately, this strategy cannot work. Since the meaning of (1) does not strictly coincide with that of (2) the two propositions will have different properties. This in itself would be unproblematic if natural language were not rich enough to express these differences. But unfortunately it is, and we can see this when we embed the sentences in a context of propositional attitude as is done in (3) and (4) below. Since (1) and (2) get the same semantical value in the classical system, sentences (3) and (4) are treated as being equivalent too. But Mary may believe (1) without believing anything about Bill at all and so, in particular, without believing (2); that is (3) may be true while (4) is false.

(3)   Mary believes that John walks

(4)   Mary believes that John walks and Bill talks or does not talk

So, here we are faced with a case where Montague Grammar does not only give wrong predictions about the notion of strict synonymy but where it also fails to account for the natural relation of logical consequence. Similarly, since (1) and (2) are treated as equivalent, by Compositionality (5) and (6) must be too.

(5)   Mary sees John walk

(6)   Mary sees John walk and Bill talk or not talk

But (6) entails that Mary sees Bill, while (5) clearly does not. Again, a wrong prediction about strict synonymy leads to a wrong prediction about entailment. We cannot content ourselves with an imperfect approximation of the relation of synonymy, since such an imperfection will immediately and necessarily lead to further imperfections in the way the relation of logical consequence is treated.

Again, the introduction of partiality helps. For if we allow sentences to be neither true nor false, then (1) and (2) will no longer be equivalent and neither the two pairs (3) and (4) and (5) and (6) will be. For example, if Mary does not see Bill at all, then the sentence 'Bill talks' will be undefined, that is, neither true nor false, in the part of the world that is seen by her and as a consequence we may take it that 'Bill talks or does not talk' and (2) are both undefined in that situation as well. Of course, (1) may still be true in that situation and so we find that in a partial logic (2) no longer follows from (1). Thus the introduction of partiality leads to a more fine-grained notion of entailment. Co-entailment in a partial theory will be a better approximation to synonymy in natural language than classical co-entailment is.

Readers will recognize some of the arguments of Barwise 1981 and Barwise and Perry 1983 in favour of (an early version of) their theory of 'Situation Semantics' here and indeed it might be said that the semantic theory that is to be developed in this book is a form of Situation Semantics, for I replace the usual concept of a possible world with that of a partial possible world—a situation. But there is an important difference between the Barwise and Perry theory and mine: while these authors are revolutionary and seek to replace Montague Grammar by their new theory, my approach is evolutionary. I do not want to abandon Montague Grammar, I want to reform it. I think we simply have not exploited Montague's paradigm to the full as yet.

There are a lot of theories that differ only minimally from Montague's original theory. These theories in their turn will have neighbours that differ only minimally from them; these will have neighbours too, and so on and so on. Some of these theories will fit the facts better than others and some will be simpler than others. Together they form a space that is *terra incognita* to us. It is the logician's task to map this unknown territory and to choose between the alternatives that are emerging. In this way we can travel a space of theories, hopefully in the direction of that golden—and, in all probability, unattainable—one that fits the facts completely. But we must proceed stepwise and each choice must be argued for carefully, lest we reject the good with the bad. It is a stepwise gradual improvement that eventually will win the day.

This book aims at making a contribution to this reformist program. I want to introduce partiality into Montague's theory. It has been suggested that this is a very difficult, if not impossible task,[1] but I do not think that it is. Indeed, I claim that the theory that is presented here is essentially *simple*. It is a generalization of a simplification of Montague's original theory. I have aimed at making the theory as compact and as explicit

---

[1] For example by Barwise who makes the following remarks in Barwise and Perry 1985: It is true that some writers have augmented the theory of possible worlds to add partial possible worlds. However, no one, as far as I know, [...] has worked out the higher-order Montague-like analogue of this theory. I thought about it once. The idea would be to have a part-of relation between partial worlds and look at those higher-type functions that were hereditarily consistent with respect to this part-of relation. However, I found that it became terribly complex once you went beyond the first couple of levels in the type hierarchy, much more complicated than the analogous problem in the theory of partial functions of higher type recursion theory.

as the theory it generalizes; I have also aimed at making it thoroughly compositional.

The book is divided into nine chapters. You are now nearing the end of the first one. In the next three chapters I give a reformulation of standard Montague Grammar, get rid of some idiosyncracies of the original and obtain a system that lends itself better to the generalization that I have in mind. But I shall prove that my reformulation is inessential and that the original relation of entailment on Montague's fragment of English is retained. Chapter 5 deals with partializations of ordinary propositional logic and predicate logic. I obtain variants of these logics that are rather close to the originals. Partial predicate logic, for example, shares many useful meta-mathematical properties (such as Compactness, recursive axiomatizability and the Löwenheim-Skolem property) with standard predicate logic, as can be seen with the help of a simple embedding of the former theory into the latter.

In Chapter 6, I generalize partial predicate logic to a partial variant of the full theory of types. After our reformulation of standard type theory in Chapter 2 this offers no particular difficulties. Again, it can be shown that many important metamathematical properties are retained, in particular Henkin's Generalized Completeness proof is not lost, although some modification is necessary. The logic is weaker, more fine-grained, than standard type theory is (when restricted to the expressions of the latter theory) and irrelevant entailments such as the ones discussed above are ruled out.

In Chapter 7, I take a closer look at the models of the new logic. It turns out that where once there were completely defined possible worlds, there now are partially specified situations. I order these by a natural 'part-of' relation and study the behaviour of English expressions with respect to this relation; in particular the question which English sentences persist under this relation is interesting. In this chapter I also argue that, apart from the relation of strong consequence given by the partial logic, a relation of weak consequence (weaker than the strong relation, but still stronger than the classical one) is needed. This particular relation is to be the explication of the consequence relation in natural language.

In Chapter 8, I give a treatment of the propositional attitudes and of the neutral perception verbs, not unlike Barwise and Perry's treatment. In fact, I have not tried to give an original account of the semantics of these constructions. I have restricted myself to showing something of a more theoretical nature: that analyses such as these can be carried out in the Montagovian variety of logical semantics in a natural way and that we get compact, parsimonious, and therefore attractive theories as a result.

It is often thought that the Hesperus-Phosphorus problem could benefit from a treatment with the help of a partialized semantics. In Chapter 9, I argue that this is not the case. A wide range of semantical theories (all those that are compositional and let the meaning of a name be dependent on its referent) can be shown *a priori* to suffer from this problem. There is a simple way out, however, and in this Chapter I give a theory that on the one hand is compatible with Russell's description theory of names, while on the other, since it contains the standard theory as a limiting case, it accounts for Kripke's intuitions. To me it came as a surprise that Russell's theory and Kripke's theory, on closer inspection, turn out to be compatible in at least some of their interpretations. I offer my theory as a synthesis of the two.

Some of the material in this book is rather technical. However, I am convinced that much of the content of the book is intelligible, even if the most technical material is omitted. In order not to put off readers who, although they have some background knowledge of logic, are no logicians, I have placed most of the proofs in a separate appendix.

2

Two Type Logics

Montague Grammar is a very elegant and a very simple theory of natural language semantics. Unfortunately its elegance and simplicity are obscured by a needlessly baroque formalization. This baroqueness of formalization complicates the theory so much that Barwise & Cooper 1981 can, not unreasonably, compare it with the kind of machine that the American artist Rube Goldberg is famous for:

> Montague had a certain job that he wanted to do and used whatever tools he had at hand to do it. If the product looks a bit like a Rube Goldberg machine, well, at least it works pretty well.

Among linguists the Rube Goldberg character of Montague's theory has created a general impression that the subject is 'difficult' and it would be worthwhile to streamline the theory a bit even if this would only serve the purpose of taking away this false impression. But streamlining the theory serves another goal as well, more important in the context of this book: If we cut down the theory to its bare essentials it will be easier to generalize it afterwards. Therefore we shall try our hand at some reformulation of Montague Semantics in this and in the next two chapters; our partialization of the theory in later chapters will run much smoother for it.

Montague based his semantic theory on a higher-order logic which he called IL—Intensional Logic. He defined this system as an extension of Russell's Simple Theory of Types (Russell 1908), a logic which had found its classical formulation in Church 1940. We may well conjecture that the great complexity of the logic IL is to be held responsible, at least in part, for Barwise & Cooper's remark, but in fact Montague's semantic theory can be based on much simpler logics. Gallin 1975 observes that from a formal point of view it is natural to interpret IL in a two-sorted variant of Russell's original type theory, a logic which he called TY_2. Replacing IL by this version of classical higher-order logic—a step taken in Groenendijk & Stokhof 1984, for example—already leads to a much smoother set-up of

Montague's original system. In this Chapter we shall consider TY_2 and shall give its basic definitions.

But our partialization of Montague's semantic theory in later chapters will not be based on the logic TY_2, as there is a further simplification that we want to make. The models of TY_2 are hierarchies built up from certain ground domains by the single rule that the set of all unary functions from one domain to another is itself a domain. Why only *unary* functions? Of course, in applications one generally needs functions and relations in more than one argument, but these, we are usually told, can be *coded* by unary functions. Two steps are needed to code a multi-argument relation. The first is to identify it with its characteristic function, a multi-argument function. This identification is very simple and unobjectionable. The second step is highly tricked. It is based on Schönfinkel's and Curry's observation that there is a one-to-one correspondence between multi-argument functions and certain unary functions of higher type. An ordinary three-place relation on individuals like the relation *give* is equated with its characteristic function in this set-up, which, in its turn, is identified with a function from individuals to functions from individuals to functions from individuals to truth-values.

The virtue of this approach is a certain parsimony, as some objects (relations, multi-argument functions) are replaced by others (unary functions) that are needed anyway. From a purely technical point of view there is nothing that can be said against this move. But the price, as I shall argue below, is nevertheless high and consists of an unintuitive complication of our models and an unintuitive recursive encoding of relatively simple objects by relatively complex ones. I shall therefore define a second type theory in which these unnecessary complications are done away with. This logic, which I shall call TT_2, can informally be described as consisting of the syntax of Church's type logic interpreted on the relational models of Orey 1959. A comparison between TY_2 and TT_2 at the end of this Chapter will reveal that, although the two systems have different models, the entailment relation on TT_2 is the same as that on the functional logic TY_2. As the latter is a classical logic this means that TT_2 is classical as well.

The functional type logic TY_2

An m-sorted functional type logic TY_m will have $m + 1$ basic or ground types, among which must be the type t, which stands for *truth values*. The two other ground types in Gallin's TY_2 are s, which stands for *world-time pairs*, and e, which is the type of *(possible) individuals* or *entities* (individuals which exist in some possible world at some point in time). From these basic types complex types are built up as in the following definition.

Definition 1 (TY$_2$ types) The set of TY$_2$ *types* is the smallest set of strings such that:

   i. e, s and t are TY$_2$ types;

   ii. If α and β are TY$_2$ types, then $(\alpha\beta)$ is a TY$_2$ type.

Types $\alpha\beta$ (we shall usually omit outer brackets) will be associated with functions from objects of type α to objects of type β, so that $e(e(et))$ e.g will stand for functions from individuals to functions from individuals to functions from individuals to truth-values. Models for the logic are based on hierarchies of typed domains, as defined in the following definition.

Definition 2 (TY$_2$ frames) A TY$_2$ *frame* is a set $\{D_\alpha \mid \alpha$ is a TY$_2$ type$\}$ such that $D_e \neq \emptyset$, $D_s \neq \emptyset$, $D_t = \{0,1\}$ and $D_{\alpha\beta} \subseteq \{F \mid F : D_\alpha \to D_\beta\}$ for each type $\alpha\beta$. A TY$_2$ frame is *standard* if $D_{\alpha\beta} = \{F \mid F : D_\alpha \to D_\beta\}$ for each type $\alpha\beta$.

The syntax of the logic is obtained in the following way. For each type we assume a denumerable infinity of variables of that type; we also assume for each type a countably infinite set of constants, ordered in the way of the natural numbers. From these basic expressions we build up terms inductively with the help of the usual logical connectives, quantification, lambda abstraction, application, and identity.

Definition 3 (TY$_2$ terms) Define for each TY$_2$ type a the set of (TY$_2$) terms of that type as follows.

   i. Every constant or variable of any type is a term of that type;

   ii. If φ and ψ are terms of type t (*formulae*) then $\neg\varphi$ and $(\varphi \wedge \psi)$ are formulae;

   iii. If φ is a formula and x is a variable of any type, then $\forall x\, \varphi$ is a formula;

   iv. If A is a term of type $\alpha\beta$ and B is a term of type α, then (AB) is a term of type β;

   v. If A is a term of type β and x is a variable of type α then $\lambda x\, (A)$ is a term of type $\alpha\beta$;

   vi. If A and B are terms of the same type, then $(A = B)$ is a formula;

Logical operators that are not mentioned here will have their usual definitions. Parentheses will be omitted where this can be done without creating confusion, on the understanding that association is to the left. So instead of writing $(\ldots (AB_1)\ldots B_n)$ I shall write $AB_1 \ldots B_n$. I shall freely add parentheses where this improves readability. Terms are sometimes subscripted with their types: as a metalanguage convention we may write A_α to indicate that A is of type α. These conventions will hold for all the logics to be discussed hereafter.

We can now interpret TY$_2$ terms on TY$_2$ frames provided that we stipulate how basic expressions (constants and variables) are to be interpreted.

This we do with the help of interpretation functions and assignments. An *interpretation function* I for a frame $F = \{D_\alpha\}_\alpha$ is a function having the set of all constants as its domain such that $I(c_\alpha) \in D_\alpha$ for each constant c_α of type α. A *standard model* is a tuple $\langle F, I \rangle$ where F is a standard frame and I is an interpretation function for F. An *assignment* is a function a taking variables as its arguments such that $a(x_\alpha) \in D_\alpha$ for each variable x_α of type α. If a is an assignment then we write $a[d/x]$ for the assignment a' defined by $a'(x) = d$ and $a'(y) = a(y)$ if $x \neq y$. The Tarski truth definition runs as follows.

Definition 4 (Tarski truth definition for TY_2) The *value* $|A|^{M,a}$ of a term A on a standard model $M = \langle F, I \rangle$ under an assignment a is defined in the following way (we sometimes write $|A|$ for $|A|^{M,a}$ and use the Von Neumann definition of 0 and 1, so $0 = \emptyset$ and $1 = \{\emptyset\}$):

i. $|c| = I(c)$ if c is a constant;
$|x| = a(x)$ if x is a variable;

ii. $|\neg\varphi| = 1 - |\varphi|$;
$|\varphi \wedge \psi| = |\varphi| \cap |\psi|$;

iii. $|\forall x_\alpha\, \varphi|^{M,a} = \bigcap_{d \in D_\alpha} |\varphi|^{M,a[d/x]}$;

iv. $|AB| = |A|(|B|)$;

v. $|\lambda x_\beta\, A|^{M,a} = $ the function F with domain D_β such that for all $d \in D_\beta$, $F(d) = |A|^{M,a[d/x]}$;

vi. $|A = B| = 1$ if $|A| = |B|$,
$= 0$ if $|A| \neq |B|$.

For reasons that will become clear in later chapters, I have taken care to couch clauses ii. and iii. completely in terms of the Boolean operations on $\{0, 1\}$, but it is clear that these clauses correspond to the usual ones. The definition of the entailment relation is also put in terms of the natural Boolean algebra on $\{0, 1\}$.

Definition 5 Let Γ and Δ be sets of TY_2 formulae. Γ *s-entails* Δ, $\Gamma \models_s \Delta$, if, for all standard models M and assignments a to M:

$$\bigcap_{\varphi \in \Gamma} |\varphi|^{M,a} \subseteq \bigcup_{\psi \in \Delta} |\psi|^{M,a}$$

A formula φ is *standardly valid* or *s-valid* if $\models_s \varphi$.

This logic behaves classically. The following schemata are s-valid, for example.

(Extensionality) $\forall x\, (Ax = Bx) \rightarrow A = B$

(Universal Instantiation) $\forall x_\alpha\, \varphi \rightarrow [A_\alpha/x]\varphi$

(Lambda Conversion) $\lambda x\, (A)B = [B/x]A$

(Leibniz's Law) $A = B \rightarrow ([A/x]\varphi \rightarrow [B/x]\varphi)$

Of course these laws (except the first) are subject to a substitutability provision: in the second schema A must be free for x in φ, in the third B must be free for x in A and in the fourth both A and B must be free for x in φ. For the proof theory of TY_2 and its one-sorted and zero-sorted variants, and for a wealth of other information about the logic, see Henkin 1950, 1963, Gallin 1975 or Andrews 1986.

This ends our discussion of TY_2 proper. But since we have decided that indices (elements of D_s) are to be interpreted as world-time pairs, we must ensure that the ground domains D_s of our models will behave in the correct way. This we enforce with the help of some non-logical axioms. Let $\approx$ and $<$ be two TY_2 constants of type $s(st)$. A formula $i \approx j$ (we use infix notation here) is to be interpreted as 'i and j have the same world component', a formula $i < j$ as 'the time component of i precedes that of j'. As the reader may like to verify, the following eight axioms make the domain D_s of indices behave like the Cartesian product of two sets, the second of which is linearly ordered.[1]

AX1 $\forall i\, i \approx i$

AX2 $\forall i \forall j\, (i \approx j \rightarrow j \approx i)$

AX3 $\forall i \forall j \forall k\, (i \approx j \rightarrow (j \approx k \rightarrow i \approx k))$

AX4 $\forall i\, \neg i < i$

AX5 $\forall i \forall j \forall k\, (i < j \rightarrow (j < k \rightarrow i < k))$

AX6 $\forall i \forall j\, (i < j \rightarrow \forall k\, (i < k \lor k < j))$

AX7 $\forall i \forall j \exists k\, (i \approx k \land \neg j < k \land \neg k < j)$

AX8 $\forall i \forall j\, ((i \approx j \land \neg j < i \land \neg i < j) \rightarrow i = j)$

It is worth noting that if we had worked with a three-sorted logic, with two separate sorts for possible worlds and times instead of our single sort of world-time pairs s, we could have made do with less axioms here. As the sole purpose of our axioms is to make indices behave as if they were pairs with a strict linear ordering on their second elements, a set of axioms saying that $<$ is a strict linear order on the domain of times would have sufficed then. We see that the number of basic types can be traded off against the number of axioms here and we have opted for fewer types as this gives an overall simplification of the theory.[2]

---

[1] For a proof of this statement see the proof of Theorem 2 in Chapter 3.

[2] As we want to prove (in Chapter 4) that our simplified set-up of Montague Grammar is equivalent to Montague's original one, the present treatment of times as points ordered by a relation of precedence is kept strictly in agreement with Montague's views. For the author's views on tense see Muskens 1995.

The relational type logic TT$_2$

The logic TY$_2$ can be said to be universal in the sense that all relations and functions over its ground domains, all relations between such functions and relations, and so on, are encodable as objects in its complex domains. A ternary relation between individuals, for example, can be represented as an object of type $e(e(et))$, and a binary relation between such ternary relations can be coded as an object of type $(e(e(et)))((e(e(et)))t)$. This is all very well, until we realise that we have coded binary relations between ternary relations as functions from functions from individuals to functions from individuals to functions from individuals to truth values to functions from functions from individuals to functions from individuals to functions from individuals to truth values to truth values. In other words, we have replaced objects that we have some intuitive grasp on by monsters that we can only reason about in an abstract way.

Moreover, if we consider type hierarchies consisting of partial rather than total functions, Schönfinkel's one-one correspondence between multi-argument functions and unary ones breaks down, as the following example, adapted from Tichy 1982, suggests: Let a be some object of type e. Consider two partial functions F_1 and F_2, both of type $e(ee)$, defined as follows: $F_1(x) = F_2(x) =$ the identity function, if $x \neq a$. $F_1(a)$ is undefined; $F_2(a)$ is defined as the ee function that is undefined for all its arguments. Clearly, $F_1 \neq F_2$. The function F_2 codes the two-place partial function F such that $F(a, y)$ is undefined and $F(x, y) = y$ if $x \neq a$. But if F_1 codes anything at all, it must code F too.

In general, I think it is not a very good idea to put intricate codifications[3] like Schönfinkel's into your logic if they are not absolutely necessary: they complicate the theory. If you confine yourself to applications of the logic you may get used to the complications; but if you are trying to prove things about the logic and try to generalize it, you will find them a hindrance to any real progress. Lambek and Scott 1981 even blame some of type theory's bad reception among mathematicians on the employment of Schönfinkel's Trick:

Type theory for the foundations of mathematics was used by Russell and Whitehead in 'Principia Mathematica'. However, it did not catch on among mathematicians, who preferred to use ad hoc methods for circumnavigating the paradoxes, as in the systems of Zermelo-Fränkel and Gödel-Bernays, even though very elegant formulations of type theory became available in the work of Church and Henkin.

---

[3]The question whether the Schönfinkel encoding is intricate or not is of course a matter of taste and opinion. Note however that a double recursion is needed if one wants to define the correspondence in any precise way. See the definition of the functions S_α in the next section.

One reason for this failure to catch on was an unwise application of Ockham's razor, which got rid of product types with the help of special tricks in one way or another. The resulting system of types, although extremely economical, was awkward to handle.

The general idea, then, is that we should first give a formulation of type theory that is not based on this identification before we can generalize it to a partial theory of types.

If you want to formalize the theory of types without making use of Schönfinkel's Trick three options are open: First, you can consider type hierarchies consisting of both multi-argument functions and multi-argument relations. This is the most general solution, but we will not need this generality in this book. Second, you may consider only multi-argument functions. Relations can then be coded by their characteristic functions. Third, you can take only relations. This is the course we shall in fact follow, since it is somewhat simpler than the first and slightly better suited to our present purposes than the second.

At first glance it might seem that the last solution is not liberal enough. In natural language semantics it is often useful to take a functional perspective on things. For example, the *intension* of an expression can fruitfully be seen as a function from possible worlds (world-time pairs) to extensions. Another example is that functional application seems to be the correct semantic correlate of many, indeed of most, syntactic constructions.

But the obvious fact that functions are indispensable need not prevent us from using only relations in setting up our logic. It is possible to view any relation as a function. Moreover, it is possible to do this in at least as many ways as the relation has argument places. The following pictures illustrate this phenomenon geometrically:

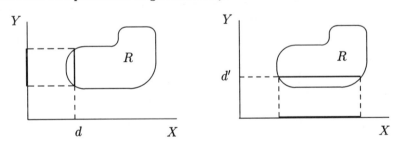

Let R be some binary relation on the reals, or, equivalently, a set of points in the Euclidean plane. With any point d on the X-axis a set of points $\{y \mid \langle d, y \rangle \in R\}$ on the Y-axis corresponds. This is illustrated in the left picture. Conversely, any d' on the Y-axis gives a set $\{x \mid \langle x, d' \rangle \in R\}$ on the X-axis, as is illustrated in the right picture. So there are two natural ways to see R as a function from the reals to the power set of the reals.

The procedure is of course entirely general:

Definition 6 (Slice Functions) Let R be an n-ary relation ($n > 0$) and let $0 < k \leq n$. Define the k-th slice function of R by:

$$F_R^k(d) = \{\langle d_1, \ldots, d_{k-1}, d_{k+1}, \ldots, d_n \rangle \mid$$
$$\langle d_1, \ldots, d_{k-1}, d, d_{k+1}, \ldots, d_n \rangle \in R\}.$$

So $F_R^k(d)$ is the $n-1$-ary relation that is obtained from R by fixing its k-th argument place by d. We shall often want to view relations as functions in this way. Note that by the usual set-theoretic definitions (remember that $\langle a \rangle = a$, $\langle \rangle = \emptyset$, $\emptyset = 0$ and $\{\emptyset\} = 1$), if R is a one-place relation, then F_R^1 is its characteristic function.

An example: Let *love* be a ternary relation, *love xyi* meaning 'y loves x at index i'. This is a relation-in-intension. Relations-in-intension are normally thought of as functions from possible worlds to extensions; F_{love}^3 is this function for *love*. On the other hand, it is natural to view the relation as the function that, when applied to an entity 'Mary' gives the property 'y loves Mary at index i'; this is the function F_{love}^1. Thus we can shift between a functional and a relational perspective without making use of Schönfinkel's identification.

A relational formulation of higher-order logic was given in Orey 1959. (See also Gallin 1975 and Van Benthem and Doets 1983.) The following two definitions give a two-sorted version of Orey's type hierarchies:

Definition 7 (TT$_2$ types) The set of types is the smallest set of strings[4] such that:

    i. e and s are types,

    ii. if $\alpha_1, \ldots, \alpha_n$ are types ($n \geq 0$), then $\langle \alpha_1 \ldots \alpha_n \rangle$ is a type.

Definition 8 (TT$_2$ frames) A *frame* is a set of sets $\{D_\alpha \mid \alpha$ is a type$\}$ such that $D_e \neq \emptyset$, $D_s \neq \emptyset$ and

$$D_{\langle \alpha_1 \ldots \alpha_n \rangle} \subseteq Pow(D_{\alpha_1} \times \ldots \times D_{\alpha_n})$$

for all types $\alpha_1, \ldots, \alpha_n$. A frame is *standard* if

$$D_{\langle \alpha_1 \ldots \alpha_n \rangle} = Pow(D_{\alpha_1} \times \ldots \times D_{\alpha_n})$$

for all $\alpha_1, \ldots, \alpha_n$.

Again domains D_e and D_s are thought to consist of possible individuals and world-time pairs respectively. Domains $D_{\langle \alpha_1 \ldots \alpha_n \rangle}$ consist of all n-ary

---

[4]A technical subtlety: types are strings of symbols over the alphabet $\{e, s, \langle, \rangle\}$, the angled brackets do not form part of the usual notation for ordered tuples. This is important since e.g. we do not want to equate the type $\langle e \rangle$ with e, while we do equate the ordered 1-tuple $\langle a \rangle$ with a.

relations having D_{α_i} as their i-th domain. Note that the string $\langle\rangle$ is a type, and that $D_{\langle\rangle} = Pow(\{\emptyset\}) = \{0,1\}$, the set of *truth-values*.

Orey used his relational frames to interpret the formulae of higher-order predicate logic on. These formulae have a syntax that is essentially that of ordinary predicate logic, be it that quantification over objects of arbitrary type is allowed. There is no lambda-abstraction and the syntax allows only one type (type $\langle\rangle$, the type of formulae) of complex expressions, while Montague Grammar assigns many different types to linguistic phrases. It is therefore clear that higher-order predicate logic as it stands does not fit our purposes. On the other hand, the syntax of ordinary functional type logic does satisfy our needs. So let us keep Church's syntax but attach Orey's models to it.

Let us see in some more detail how this can be done (see also Muskens 1989b). We need a slight reformulation of the syntax, or rather of the typing of terms. Assume for each type the existence of a denumerable infinity of variables of that type; also assume for each type a countably infinite set of constants, ordered in the way of the natural numbers, and use the following clauses to build up terms.

Definition 9 (TT$_2$ terms) Define, for each α, the set of *terms* of that type as follows.

    i. Every constant or variable of any type is a term of that type;

    ii. If φ and ψ are terms of type $\langle\rangle$ (*formulae*) then $\neg\varphi$ and $(\varphi \wedge \psi)$ are formulae;

    iii. If φ is a formula and x is a variable of any type, then $\forall x\, \varphi$ is a formula;

    iv. If A is a term of type $\langle\beta\alpha_1\ldots\alpha_n\rangle$ and B is a term of type β, then (AB) is a term of type $\langle\alpha_1\ldots\alpha_n\rangle$;

    v. If A is a term of type $\langle\alpha_1\ldots\alpha_n\rangle$ and x is a variable of type β then $\lambda x\,(A)$ is a term of type $\langle\beta\alpha_1\ldots\alpha_n\rangle$;

    vi. If A and B are terms of the same type, then $(A = B)$ is a formula.

Again we define *standard models* to be tuples $\langle F, I\rangle$, consisting of a frame $F = \{D_\alpha\}_\alpha$ and an *interpretation function* I, having the set of constants as its domain, such that $I(c) \in D_\alpha$ for each constant c of type a. *Assignments* are defined as before.

To evaluate our terms on these relational standard models we can use the slice functions defined above. We simply let the value of a term AB be the result of applying (the first slice function of) the value of A to the value of B. Terms of the form $\lambda x.\, A$ we evaluate by an inverse procedure.

Definition 10 (Tarski truth definition for TT$_2$) The *value* $\|A\|^{M,a}$ of a term A on a model M under an assignment a is defined in the following way (To improve readability I shall sometimes write $\|A\|$ for $\|A\|^{M,a}$):

    i. $\|c\| = I(c)$ if c is a constant;

$\|x\| = a(x)$ if x is a variable;

ii. $\|\neg\varphi\| = 1 - \|\varphi\|$;

$\|\varphi \wedge \psi\| = \|\varphi\| \cap \|\psi\|$;

iii. $\|\forall x_\alpha \, \varphi\|^{M,a} = \bigcap_{d \in D_\alpha} \|\varphi\|^{M,a[d/x]}$;

iv. $\|AB\| = F^1_{\|A\|}(\|B\|)$;

v. $\|\lambda x_\beta \, A\|^{M,a} =$ the R such that $F^1_R(d) = \|A\|^{M,a[d/x]}$ for all $d \in D_\beta$;

vi. $\|A = B\| = 1$ if $\|A\| = \|B\|$;

$= 0$ if $\|A\| \neq \|B\|$.

Clauses i, ii, iii and vi are completely analogous to the corresponding clauses in the corresponding definition for TY_2; only clauses iv and v differ. Note that the following identities hold.

$$
\begin{aligned}
\|AB\| &= \{\langle d_1, \ldots, d_n \rangle \mid \langle \|B\|, d_1, \ldots, d_n \rangle \in \|A\|\} \\
\|\lambda x_\beta \, A\|^{M,a} &= \{\langle d, d_1, \ldots, d_n \rangle \mid d \in D_\beta \text{ and} \\
&\quad \langle d_1, \ldots, d_n \rangle \in \|A\|^{M,a[d/x]}\}.
\end{aligned}
$$

Thanks to the Boolean character of our relational domains it is possible to define the notion of logical consequence for terms of arbitrary relational type, not only for formulae.

Definition 11 (Entailment in TT_2) Let Γ and Δ be sets of terms of some type $\alpha = \langle \alpha_1 \ldots \alpha_n \rangle$. Γ is said to *s-entail* Δ, $\Gamma \models_s \Delta$, if

$$
\bigcap_{A \in \Gamma} \|A\|^{M,a} \subseteq \bigcup_{B \in \Delta} \|B\|^{M,a}
$$

for all standard models M and assignments a to M.

The logics TY_2 and TT_2 compared

Let us compare our relational frames with the more usual functional ones. On the one hand, since every function is a relation, it should be clear that all objects occurring in some functional standard frame occur in the relational standard frame based on the same ground domains D_e and D_s as well. On the other hand we can code relations as functions by the Schönfinkel codification. Let us give a formal account of this encoding. First we need to establish a correspondence between relational types and functional ones.

Definition 12 Define the function Σ (Σ is for Schönfinkel) taking types to TY_2 types by the following double recursion:

I $\Sigma(e) = e$, $\Sigma(s) = s$

II   i. $\Sigma(\langle \rangle) = t$

      ii. $\Sigma(\langle \alpha_1 \ldots \alpha_n \rangle) = (\Sigma(\alpha_1)\Sigma(\langle \alpha_2 \ldots \alpha_n \rangle))$ if $n \geq 1$.

So, for example, $\Sigma(\langle e \rangle) = et$, $\Sigma(\langle\langle e\rangle\rangle) = (et)t$, $\Sigma(\langle ee\rangle) = e(et)$ and $\Sigma(\langle\langle se\rangle\langle se\rangle\rangle) = (s(et))((s(et))t)$. If α is the type of some relation then $\Sigma(\alpha)$ is the type of the unary function that codes this relation in functional type theory. Note that arguments of Σ tend to have less length than the corresponding values. Let us call any TY$_2$ type that is a value of Σ *quasi-relational*. It is not difficult to characterize the quasi-relational types: A TY$_2$ type is a value of Σ if and only if no occurrence of e or s immediately precedes a right bracket in it.[5]

The next step is to write out a full definition of the Schönfinkel encoding function. This function may look simple if only relations of individuals are considered. In the higher-order case however, where relations can take relations as arguments, which in their turn can again take relations as arguments and so on, the identification is somewhat less than transparent and the formal definition of the encoding function looks rather forbidding.

Definition 13 (The Schönfinkel Encoding) Let $F = \{D_\alpha \mid \alpha \text{ is a type}\}$ be a standard frame and let $F' = \{D'_\alpha \mid \alpha \text{ is a TY}_2 \text{ type}\}$ be the TY$_2$ standard frame such that $D_e = D'_e$ and $D_s = D'_s$. For each type α define a function $S_\alpha : D_\alpha \to D'_{\Sigma(\alpha)}$ by the following double recursion:

I $\quad S_e(d) = d$, if $d \in D_e$; $S_s(d) = d$, if $d \in D_s$;

II $\quad$ i. $S_{\langle\rangle}(d) = d$, if $d \in D_{\langle\rangle}$;

$\quad\quad$ ii. If $n > 0$, $\alpha = \langle\alpha_1 \ldots \alpha_n\rangle$ and $R \in D_\alpha$, then $S_\alpha(R)$ is the function G of type $(\Sigma(\alpha_1)\Sigma(\langle\alpha_2 \ldots \alpha_n\rangle))$ such that $G(f) = S_{\langle\alpha_2 \ldots \alpha_n\rangle}(F_R^1(S_{\alpha_1}^{-1}(f)))$ for each $f \in D'_{\Sigma(\alpha_1)}$.

It is easy to prove that the functions S_α are bijections. Hence the definition is correct.

This definition shows us two things. The first is that we *can* code multi-argument relations as unary functions; the functions S_α are *isomorphisms*: we have that $\langle d_1, \ldots, d_n \rangle \in R$ iff $S(R)(S(d_1)) \ldots (S(d_n)) = 1$, for all relations R (of any type) as can easily be verified. The second thing that this definition shows us is that we *shouldn't* code multi-argument relations as unary functions. Obviously, the functions S_α tend to increase complexity rather dramatically. This doubly recursive encoding is just a needless complication. If we want Montague Grammar to look a little less like a Rube Goldberg machine, we may as well skip it.

On at least one occasion the Schönfinkel encoding has led to a redundancy in semantic theory as I shall explain now. In view of the fact that natural language and, or and not can be used with expressions of almost all linguistic categories, type domains should have a Boolean structure. This has

---

[5]This characterization presupposes the 'official' notation for functional types, with outer brackets in place. For example, in order to avoid mathematical clutter we usually write se for (se), but this type is not quasi-relational.

been argued for by a variety of authors, beginning with Von Stechow 1974 (see also Keenan and Faltz 1978). Obviously, Orey's relational standard frames have a Boolean structure on all their (non-basic) domains, since they are power sets. So we can give a very simple rule for the interpretation of natural language conjunction, disjunction and negation: they are to be treated as ∩, ∪ and − (complementation within a typed domain) respectively. Entailment between expressions of the same category is to be treated as inclusion.

This does not differ much, of course, from the usual treatment of entailment and the expressions just mentioned. The point is rather that the relevant Boolean operations are not as easily available in a functional type theory as they are here. Therefore Gazdar 1980 gives some pointwise recursive definitions. Let us have a look at one of them. Before we can give it, we must characterize a certain subclass of the TY_2 types, the so-called *conjoinable* ones:

Definition 14 (Conjoinable TY_2 types)

   i. t is conjoinable;

   ii. If β is conjoinable, then $\alpha\beta$ is conjoinable.

Note that, while not all conjoinable TY_2 types are quasi-relational, there is a close kinship between the two classes of types: A TY_2 type is quasi-relational if and only if all its subtypes are either basic or conjoinable.

Having defined the conjoinable types we can define generalized conjunction in functional type theory thus:

Definition 15 (Generalized Conjunction)

   i. $a \sqcap b := a \cap b$, if $a, b \in \{0,1\}$;

   ii. If F_1 and F_2 are functions of some conjoinable TY_2 type $\alpha\beta$, then the function $F_1 \sqcap F_2$ is defined by: $(F_1 \sqcap F_2)(z) = F_1(z) \sqcap F_2(z)$, for all z of TY_2 type α.

Similar definitions can be given for generalized disjunction, complementation and inclusion (see Groenendijk and Stokhof 1984 for the last operation). But the need for these definitions is an artefact of Schönfinkels Trick; they enable us to treat generalized co-ordination by reversing its effect: It is not difficult to prove that, for any R_1, R_2 of relational type, $S(R_1 \cap R_2) = S(R_1) \sqcap S(R_2)$. As soon as we get rid of the Trick, the need for its reversals, these pointwise definitions, vanishes too. This is an example of a case where the encoding has actually generated redundant theory.

We can use the formal characterization of the Schönfinkel Encoding to prove an equivalence between our two logics. First, let us stipulate that the constants (variables) of any TT_2 type α are identical to the constants (variables) of TY_2 type $\Sigma(\alpha)$. Given this stipulation it is easily seen that all TT_2 terms of any type α are TY_2 terms of type $\Sigma(\alpha)$ (and vice versa). So our new syntax is just a part of the TY_2 syntax. Of course not all TY_2 terms are TT_2 terms by this identification since Σ is not onto, but the TY_2 terms that belong to TT_2 are exactly those whose subterms are all of a quasi-relational type.

The following theorem says that on TT_2 sentences both logics give the same entailment relation. This means that we can have it both ways; we can have the nice models of the relational theory but we do not have to give up the classical entailment relation. In particular, laws such as Extensionality, Lambda Conversion, Universal Instantiation and Leibniz's Law continue to hold.

Theorem 1 *Let* Γ *and* Δ *be sets of* TT_2 *sentences then* $\Gamma \models_s \Delta$ *in* TT_2 *iff* $\Gamma \models_s \Delta$ *in* TY_2.

The proof is in the Appendix.

3

The Logic IL

Montague originally based his semantics on the logic IL, a higher order logic enriched with modal and temporal operators, and since we want to be able to compare our approach with Montague's and prove (in the next Chapter) that the two approaches are in fact equivalent, we need to review his logic in a little detail.[1] We shall give its main definitions, discuss the logic and compare it with the logics that were introduced in Chapter 2.[2] It will turn out that IL can be embedded within TY_2 and that an important part of IL can be embedded within our relational type theory TT_2, provided that the world-time pair axioms AX1, ..., AX8 are adopted.

The logic IL is a typed system, just as the classical logics that were considered in the previous Chapter. The following is a definition of its types.

Definition 16 (IL types) The set of IL types is the smallest set of strings such that:

   i. e and t are IL types;

   ii. If α and β are IL types, then $(\alpha\beta)$ is an IL type;

   iii. If α is an IL type, then $(s\alpha)$ is an IL type.

It is clear from this definition that all IL types are TY_2 types, but the TY_2 type s, for example, is not an IL type. For each type, we again assume the existence of a denumerable infinity of variables and countably many constants, both sets indexed by the natural numbers. The terms of IL are built up as those of TY_2, but modal and temporal operators ˆ, ˇ, □, F and P are added. ˆA is to be interpreted as the *intension* of A (a function from indices, or world-time pairs, to the values of A at those indices), while

---

[1] This Chapter can be skipped on a first reading by those readers who are also prepared to skip the proof of next Chapter's Theorem 3. The rest of the book does not presuppose any of the material presented here.

[2] For more information about IL and its application in the semantics of natural language consult Montague 1974, Gallin 1975, Dowty et al. 1981, Gamut 1991 or Chierchia and McConnell-Ginet 1991.

$\check{\ }A$ gives the value of A at the current index; $\Box$ is the necessity operator, universal quantification over world-time pairs, while F ('Future') and P ('Past') are operators that are to be interpreted as quantifying over times.

Definition 17 (IL terms) Define for each IL type α the set of IL terms of that type as follows.

    i. Every constant or variable of any type is a term of that type;

    ii. If φ and ψ are terms of type t (*formulae*) then $\neg\varphi$ and $(\varphi \wedge \psi)$ are formulae;

    iii. If φ is a formula and x is a variable of any type, then $\forall x\, \varphi$ is a formula;

    iv. If A is a term of type $\alpha\beta$ and B is a term of type α, then (AB) is a term of type β;

    v. If A is a term of type β and x is a variable of type α then $\lambda x\,(A)$ is a term of type $\alpha\beta$;

    vi. If A and B are terms of the same type, then $(A = B)$ is a formula;

    vii. If A is a term of type α, then $\hat{\ }(A)$ is a term of type $s\alpha$;

    viii. If A is a term of type $s\alpha$, then $\check{\ }(A)$ is a term of type α;

    ix. If φ is a formula then $\Box\varphi$ is a formula;

    x. If φ is a formula then $F\varphi$ and $P\varphi$ are formulae.

A *model* for IL is a quintuple $\langle D, W, T, <, I\rangle$ such that D, W and T are non-empty sets, $<$ is a linear ordering of T and I is an interpretation function with the set of all constants as its domain, such that $I(c_\alpha) \in D_{s\alpha}$ for each constant c_α of type α, where the sets D_α are defined using the following induction.

$$
\begin{aligned}
D_e &= D \\
D_t &= \{0, 1\} \\
D_{\alpha\beta} &= \{F \mid F : D_\alpha \to D_\beta\} \\
D_{s\alpha} &= \{F \mid F : W \times T \to D_\alpha\}.
\end{aligned}
$$

Intuitively, we interpret D as a domain of possible individuals, W as a set of possible worlds, T as a set of points in time and $<$ as the relation of temporal precedence on that set. *Assignments* and the notation $a[d/x]$ are defined as usual.

    Terms are evaluated on models with the help of a (rather formidable looking) Tarski-style truth definition.

Definition 18 (Tarski truth definition for IL) The *value* $\|A\|^{M,w,t,a}$ of a term A on a model $M = \langle D, W, T, <, I\rangle$ in world $w \in W$ at time $t \in T$ under an assignment a is defined in the following way (I shall sometimes write $\|A\|$ for $\|A\|^{M,w,t,a}$):

    i. $\|c\| = I(c)(\langle w, t\rangle)$ if c is a constant;
    $\|x\| = a(x)$ if x is a variable;

ii. $\|\neg\varphi\| = 1$ iff $\|\varphi\| = 0$;
$\|\varphi \wedge \psi\| = 1$ iff $\|\varphi\| = 1$ and $\|\psi\| = 1$;

iii. $\|\forall x_\alpha \varphi\|^{M,w,t,a} = 1$ iff $\|\varphi\|^{M,w,t,a[d/x]} = 1$ for all $d \in D_\alpha$;

iv. $\|AB\| = \|A\|(\|B\|)$;

v. $\|\lambda x_\beta A\|^{M,w,t,a} =$ the function F with domain D_β such that for all $d \in D_\beta : F(d) = \|A\|^{M,w,t,a[d/x]}$;

vi. $\|A = B\| = 1$ iff $\|A\| = \|B\|$;

vii. $\|{}^\wedge A\|^{M,w,t,a} =$ the function F with domain $W \times T$ such that for all $\langle w', t' \rangle \in W \times T : F(\langle w', t' \rangle) = \|A\|^{M,w',t',a}$;

viii. $\|{}^\vee A\|^{M,w,t,a} = \|A\|^{M,w,t,a}(\langle w, t \rangle)$;

ix. $\|\Box\varphi\|^{M,w,t,a} = 1$ iff $\|\varphi\|^{M,w',t',a} = 1$ for all $w' \in W$ and $t' \in T$;

x. $\|F\varphi\|^{M,w,t,a} = 1$ iff $\|\varphi\|^{M,w,t',a} = 1$ for some $t' \in T$ such that $t < t'$;
$\|P\varphi\|^{M,w,t,a} = 1$ iff $\|\varphi\|^{M,w,t',a} = 1$ for some $t' \in T$ such that $t' < t$.

Note the special treatment of the non-logical constants in the first clause of this definition: constants of type α are interpreted as functions of type $s\alpha$ by the interpretation function I but these functions are applied to the current world-time pair to get the actual value, an object which is of type α again.

We say that a formula φ is *true* in some model M in world w at time t under an assignment a if $\|\varphi\|^{M,w,t,a} = 1$. The notion of entailment is defined as follows.

Definition 19 Let Γ and Δ be sets of IL formulae. Γ *entails* Δ, $\Gamma \models_s \Delta$, if, for all models $M = \langle D, W, T, <, I \rangle$, worlds $w \in W$, times $t \in T$ and assignments a to M, if $\|\varphi\|^{M,w,t,a} = 1$ for all $\varphi \in \Gamma$ then $\|\psi\|^{M,w,t,a} = 1$ for some $\psi \in \Delta$.

A formula φ is called *valid* if $\models_s \varphi$. Here is a schema that is valid.

(7) $\forall x (Ax = Bx) \to A = B$

Since this is the axiom of Extensionality we may fairly say that Intensional Logic is an extensional logic. Here are some formulae that are *not* valid.

(8) $\forall x \exists y \Box(x = y) \to \exists y \Box(c = y)$

(9) $\lambda p_t (Fp)P(c_1 = c_2) = FP(c_1 = c_2)$

(10) $c_1 = c_2 \to (\Box(c_1 = c_1) \to \Box(c_1 = c_2))$

So while IL contains the symbol $\forall$, we do not have Universal Instantiation; while there is a λ, Beta Conversion does not hold, and while there is a symbol $=$, this symbol does not conform to Leibniz's Law, the principle that says that equals can be substituted for equals. This is rather bad, as Universal Instantiation seems to be an essential part of the meaning of universal quantification, and Beta Conversion and Leibniz's Law likewise seem to be essential to the meaning of λ and $=$ respectively.

There are restricted versions of these logical laws however. Call a term *modally closed* if it is built up from variables and terms of the form $\hat{\ }A$ or $\Box\varphi$ with the help of $\forall$, λ, $=$, $\neg$, $\wedge$ and application. We have that $\lambda x\,(A)B = [B/x]A$ *provided that*

   i. B is free for x in A; and

   ii. (a) no free occurrence of x in A lies within the scope of F, P, $\Box$ or $\hat{\ }$; or

      (b) B is modally closed.

Similarly restricted versions of Universal Instantiation and Leibniz's Law also hold. But all these restrictions make the logic less than transparent and one might well wonder what is going on.

Worse, as Friedman and Warren 1980 remark, IL does not have the Church-Rosser (or 'diamond') property if we employ this restricted version of Beta Conversion (see also Janssen 1983). It is well known that ordinary type logic has this property: Given any term, we can, using Beta Conversion and renaming of bound variables ('Alpha Conversion'), simplify all subterms of the form $\lambda x\,(A)B$ ('redexes') to the form $[B/x]A$. The order in which we reduce redexes is immaterial; whatever order we choose, we end up with the same term (modulo Alpha Conversion). This property does not hold for IL, not even when we restrict ourselves to redexes that satisfy condition ii. above. Friedman and Warren give the following example. Consider the term

(11) $\lambda x\,(\lambda y\,(\hat{\ }y = f(x))x)c,$

where x and y are variables of some type α, c is a constant of that type and f is a variable of type $\alpha(s\alpha)$. Two reductions are possible. We can reduce to the term

(12) $\lambda y\,(\hat{\ }y = f(c))c,$

which with the present restrictions cannot be reduced any further. We can also reduce the inner redex in order to obtain

(13) $\lambda x\,(\hat{\ }x = f(x))c,$

and this term neither can be simplified any further. Hence there is no term to which (12) and (13) both reduce.

This failure of the diamond property should make us extremely reluctant to base our semantic theories on the logic IL, as it is theoretically possible that an IL term that we need in practice may reduce to two different terms that cannot themselves be reduced and this in its turn could make it very hard to decide whether one sentence follows from another according to the theory. So far, no examples of such terms have propped op in practical work, but there is no guarantee that this will never happen.

Why does IL show such exotic behaviour; why do Leibniz's Law, Universal Instantiation and Beta Conversion not hold under the normal conditions? Because the logic was explicitly designed to reflect certain opacity phenomena in natural language. To take an example, the sentences *Sara is Miss America* and *Necessarily Sara is Sara* do not entail the sentence *Necessarily Sara is Miss America*; and so, it is argued, (10) should not be valid (there is a similar argument against Universal Instantiation). According to this view, the inelegancies of IL should be weighed against the fact that the logic truly reflects natural language in an important respect.

But there is an objection against this argument that derives from the nature of our trade. We are doing semantics, that is, we are after a theory of meaning for natural language. The subject matter of our theory, then, is *meanings* and identity in our theory is most naturally interpreted as identity of meaning, or *synonymy*. Although the sentence *Sara is Miss America* may certainly be called an identity statement in a certain sense, as it expresses that Sara is identical to Miss America *at the present moment of time and in the present world*, it does not follow that the word *is* should be rendered as $=$. The word simply does not express synonymy, it expresses *coreference* and the sentence expresses the fact that the two names happen to have the same bearer in the present situation. Opacity phenomena in natural language are no counterexamples to Leibniz's Law, they merely illustrate that the forms of the verb *be* do not express identity of meaning (although they do express identity of reference).

Instead of giving up Leibniz's Law, we decide to take it seriously. If expressions stand for the same thing, they are interchangeable in all contexts. It follows that the expressions *Sara* and *Miss America*, that are clearly not interchangeable in modal or temporal contexts, cannot have the same semantic value. Expressions stand for their meanings, not for their references. Therefore it is wrong to translate *Sara is Miss America* as an identity statement. It may be true that Sara is Miss America but it is certainly false that *Sara* means *Miss America*. This point of view leads us away from the ideas behind the logic IL but it is not in conflict with possible worlds semantics as such, for we can continue to treat the meaning of a sentence as a set of indices, the meaning of an intransitive verb as a function from indices to sets of entities and so on.

We now turn to a translation from IL into the much more perspicuous logic TY_2. This translation was first given by Daniel Gallin in 1975, but we shall extend it slightly: Gallin defined a version of IL in which the temporal operators P and F did not occur and then embedded this version into the two-sorted logic; we shall repeat the construction for the full version of IL.

Definition 20 (Gallin's Embedding) Let i be some fixed TY_2 variable of type s. The function $^\bullet$, sending IL terms to TY_2 terms, is defined with the help of the following clauses:

  i. $x^\bullet = x$, if x is a variable

$c^\bullet = ki$, where k is the n-th constant of type $s\alpha$, if c is the n-th constant of type α.

ii. $(\varphi \wedge \psi)^\bullet = \varphi^\bullet \wedge \psi^\bullet$
   $(\neg\varphi)^\bullet = \neg\varphi^\bullet$

iii. $(\forall x\, \varphi)^\bullet = \forall x\, \varphi^\bullet$

iv. $(AB)^\bullet = A^\bullet B^\bullet$

v. $(\lambda x\, A)^\bullet = \lambda x\, A^\bullet$

vi. $(A = B)^\bullet = (A^\bullet = B^\bullet)$

vii. $(\hat{\,}A)^\bullet = \lambda i\, A^\bullet$

viii. $(\check{\,}A)^\bullet = A^\bullet i$

ix. $(\Box\varphi)^\bullet = \forall i\, \varphi^\bullet$

x. $(F\varphi)^\bullet = \exists j\, (i < j \wedge i \approx j \wedge [j/i]\varphi^\bullet)$
   $(P\varphi)^\bullet = \exists j\, (j < i \wedge i \approx j \wedge [j/i]\varphi^\bullet)$

Given our world-time pair axioms, an IL term A and its translation $A^\bullet$ will behave exactly alike, which means that the translation is meaning preserving.

Theorem 2 *Let Γ and Δ be sets of IL formulae; let $\Gamma^\bullet$ and $\Delta^\bullet$ be the sets $\{\varphi^\bullet \mid \varphi \in \Gamma\}$ and $\{\varphi^\bullet \mid \varphi \in \Delta\}$ respectively, then:*

$$\Gamma \models_s \Delta \ \text{in IL iff } \Gamma^\bullet, \text{AX1}, \ldots, \text{AX8} \models_s \Delta^\bullet \ \text{in TY}_2.$$

A proof of this theorem can be found in the Appendix.

In Gallin's Embedding the fixed type s variable i plays the role of the current index in IL and the operations $\hat{\,}$, $\check{\,}$ and $\Box$ are reduced to abstraction, application to i and universal quantification respectively. The tense operators F and P are translated into certain restricted forms of existential quantification. Note that while IL treats the tense operators as logical operators, they are translated with the help of non-logical constants that obey certain non-logical axioms here. This means that we have relieved the logic of the task of providing the structure that is needed for the interpretation of tense, a job that we have transferred to the non-logical part of the system. As a result the logic is kept pure. A practical consequence of this move is a greater modularity: should we want to change our temporal ontology, replacing moments of time by intervals for example, we can simply change the axioms AX1, ..., AX8; there is no need to fuss with the underlying logic.

Gallin's embedding helps us to see why Beta Conversion, Universal Instantiation and Leibniz's Law are subject to such strange restrictions in IL. Constants in IL are of a mixed character: in fact they can be viewed as constants carrying a hidden variable with them. The operators $\check{\,}$, F and P also introduce ghost variables. On the other hand $\hat{\,}$, $\Box$, F and P are capable of binding these variables. It is not difficult to see that the translation $B^\bullet$ of a term B will contain free occurrences of the variable i if and only if B is not modally closed; these occurrences will get bound if $B^\bullet$ is substituted for x in $A^\bullet$ if and only if some occurrence of x in A is in the scope of $\hat{\ }$, $\Box$, F or P. Hence the restrictions.

It is also instructive to reconsider Friedman and Warren's example to the effect that restricted Beta Conversion in IL is not Church-Rosser (again compare Janssen 1983). The TY_2 translation of (11) is

(14) $\lambda x \,(\lambda y \,(\lambda i \,(y) = f(x))x)ki,$

where k is the n-th constant of type $s\alpha$, if c is the n-th constant of type α. Reduction of the outer redex gives

(15) $\lambda y \,(\lambda i \,(y) = f(ki))ki,$

the translation of (12). Reducing the inner redex gives

(16) $\lambda x \,(\lambda i \,(x) = f(x))ki,$

which is (13)'s translation. But this time further reductions are possible: via Alpha Conversion and Beta Conversion both terms reduce to

(17) $\lambda j \,(ki) = f(ki).$

Now we see why IL is not Church-Rosser: since IL hides certain bound variables we cannot rename them; we can apply Alpha Conversion to $\lambda i \,(y)$ in order to get $\lambda j \,(y)$; but since in $\hat{\ }y$ no bound variable is shown, Alpha Conversion is inapplicable.

The *Sara is Miss America* example gets a similar analysis. Note that (10) is translated as (18) below by Gallin's Embedding. This time *Sara* and *Miss America* are rendered as the $s\alpha$ constants k_1 and k_2 respectively and the sentence expresses that if the referents of *Sara* and *Miss America* are the same at the actual index i (and the referent of *Sara* at each index is self-identical), they must be the same at all indices. This is clearly not valid. (18) formalises the original *Sara is Miss America* argument just as well as (10) does, but this slightly more explicit formalisation allows us to account for the invalidity of the reasoning without any violation of Leibniz's Law.

(18) $k_1 i = k_2 i \rightarrow (\forall i \,(k_1 i = k_1 i) \rightarrow \forall i \,(k_1 i = k_2 i)).$

From Gallin's embedding theorem we see that we can replace IL with TY_2 when doing Montague Semantics. Instead of translating a natural language expression to an IL term A we can translate it to $A^\bullet$. The result will be a logic that is more manageable and one in which the logical operators have their familiar classical properties. We also obtain a somewhat greater expressivity: not all TY_2 terms are equivalent to a value of $^\bullet$. There may be empirical reasons to want this added expressivity. For example, Groenendijk and Stokhof 1984 argue that the meaning of a question generally is of the form $\lambda i \lambda j \varphi$, where φ is a formula. In our notation, they render the meaning of Does John love Mary? as (19), for example.

(19) $\lambda i \lambda j$ (*love mary john i = love mary john j*)

Applied to an index i where it is in fact the case that John loves Mary this term will give the proposition that John loves Mary; application to an index where this is not the case gives the proposition that John does not love Mary.

Equivalence relations over the domain of world-time pairs such as the one denoted by (19) are not expressible within IL, however. Since $^{\bullet}$-translations of IL terms can abstract over *one* variable of type s only, this term is outside the range of Gallin's Embedding.

The embedding we have discussed here sends IL to TY_2, but since the terms of our relational logic TT_2 are identical to certain terms of TY_2, it also sends part of IL into that logic. In the previous Chapter we have characterized the TY_2 terms that are also TT_2 terms as those terms whose subterms are of quasi-relational type, or, in other words, as those terms that have no subterm of a type in which a right parenthesis is immediately preceded by an e or an s. Since the translation $^{\bullet}$ preserves types and in view of Theorem 1 we have the following Corollary to Gallin's Embedding.

Corollary. *Let* Γ *and* Δ *be sets of IL formulae which do not contain constants of type* e *and all of whose subterms have quasi-relational types; let* $\Gamma^{\bullet}$ *and* $\Delta^{\bullet}$ *be the sets* $\{\varphi^{\bullet} \mid \varphi \in \Gamma\}$ *and* $\{\varphi^{\bullet} \mid \varphi \in \Delta\}$ *respectively, then:*

$$\Gamma \models_s \Delta \text{ in IL iff } \Gamma^{\bullet}, AX1, \ldots, AX8 \models_s \Delta^{\bullet} \text{ in } TT_2.$$

4

PTQ Revisited

Montague's PTQ article (Montague 1973), the paper in which he gave his 'Proper Treatment of Quantification', functions as the paradigm of Montague Grammar. In this paper a fragment of ordinary English was provided with a semantics, via a translation into the logic IL. In this Chapter we shall take a second look at the PTQ fragment, reformulate its syntax and give it a simplified semantics on the basis of our relational type logic TT_2.

The set-up of the Chapter is as follows. We shall first define certain structures called *analysis trees*. Languages are ambiguous and expressions may have more than one reading; analysis trees represent those readings. As a second step we shall give an inductive assignment of *phrases* to analysis trees. If a phrase is assigned to an analysis tree, the tree will be a reading of that phrase. Thirdly, analysis trees will be translated into TT_2 by a separate induction. This will associate truth conditions and other semantic values with trees and will induce a relation of entailment on them. If a tree with certain truth conditions functions as a possible reading of a sentence we can say that the sentence has those truth conditions, given that particular reading. It will also be possible to characterize an argument as valid or invalid, given readings of its premises and conclusion. The relation of entailment that is induced on the fragment by this procedure is provably orthodox: we shall show that it equals the entailment relation given in the text book Dowty et al. 1981 (DWP).[1]

---

[1] The main difference between Montague's own semantics for the PTQ fragment and that given in DWP concerns the use of 'individual concepts' (type *se* functions). Montague employed these in order to circumvent certain difficulties with sentences like Partee's *The temperature is ninety but it is rising*, but DWP skip the use of individual concepts altogether, following Bennett 1974, who saw that these did not only complicate the theory considerably, but moreover created as many problems as they were supposed to solve. For a careful discussion see DWP; for a contrary opinion Janssen 1984.

We accept Bennett's Simplification here. However, it is possible to reintroduce individual concepts in the present relational setting by treating them as ⟨se⟩ type relations that happen to be functional. See also Chapter 9 where individual concepts are reintroduced in a somewhat different manner.

Categories and Analysis Trees

The system we are describing here is a form of categorial grammar and all syntactic objects are required to have some category, just as all objects in type logic are subsumed under some type. The set of categories is defined in the following way.

Definition 21 (Categories)

    i. E is a category; S is a category;

    ii. If A and B are categories and $A \neq E$, then A/B and $A//B$ are categories.

The idea here is that an object of category A/B or category $A//B$ combines with an object of category B to an object of category A. For example, if Mary is assigned to category $S/(S/E)$ and run is given category S/E, then the two expressions can combine into Mary runs. Definition 23 below will specify more modes of combination, but this is the main idea.

Table 1 lists the categories that we shall actually use, the way in which we abbreviate these categories and the traditional name that is connected to them.

Category A	Abbreviation	Traditional name
S		Sentence
S/E	IV	Verb Phrase/Intransitive Verb
$S//E$	CN	Common Noun
S/S		Sentence Adverb
S/IV	T or NP	Noun Phrase/Proper Name
IV/S		Sentence-complement Verb
IV/IV	IAV	Verb Phrase Adverb
$IV//IV$		Infinitive-complement Verb
IV/T	TV	Transitive Verb
T/CN	DET	Determiner
IAV/T		Preposition

TABLE 1

The next step is to define the lexicon of our fragment. Each category A comes with a set of basic expressions B_A.

Definition 22 (Basic Expressions)

$$B_{IV} = \{\text{run}, \text{walk}, \text{talk}\}$$
$$B_{CN} = \{\text{man}, \text{woman}, \text{park}, \text{fish}, \text{pen}, \text{unicorn}\}$$
$$B_{S/S} = \{\text{necessarily}\}$$
$$B_T = \{\text{John}, \text{Mary}, \text{Bill}, \text{he}_0, \text{he}_1, \text{he}_2, \ldots\}$$

$$B_{IV/S} = \{\text{believe that, assert that}\}$$
$$B_{IAV} = \{\text{rapidly, slowly, voluntarily, allegedly}\}$$
$$B_{IV//IV} = \{\text{try to, wish to}\}$$
$$B_{TV} = \{\text{find, lose, eat, love, date, be, seek, conceive}\}$$
$$B_{DET} = \{\text{every, the, a}\}$$
$$B_{IAV/T} = \{\text{in, about}\}$$
$$B_A = \emptyset \text{ if } A \text{ is any category other than those mentioned above.}$$

The words in this lexicon can be combined into larger units according to certain modes of combination. Each clause in the definition below corresponds to such a mode of combination, but the analysis trees which are defined here are still devoid of syntactic and semantic information. Analysis trees summarize the basic combinatorics of an expression.

Definition 23 (Analysis Trees) For each category A the set AT_A of *analysis trees* of category A is defined as follows.

Basic rule

G1. $B_A \subseteq AT_A$ for every category A.

Relative clause rule. For each natural number n:

G2. If $\xi \in AT_{CN}$ and $\vartheta \in AT_S$ then $[\xi\vartheta]^{2,n} \in AT_{CN}$.

Rules of functional application

G3. If $\xi \in AT_{DET}$ and $\vartheta \in AT_{CN}$ then $[\xi\vartheta]^3 \in AT_T$.

G4. If $\xi \in AT_T$ and $\vartheta \in AT_{IV}$ then $[\xi\vartheta]^4 \in AT_t$.

G5. If $\xi \in AT_{TV}$ and $\vartheta \in AT_T$ then $[\xi\vartheta]^5 \in AT_{IV}$.

G6. If $\xi \in AT_{IAV/T}$ and $\vartheta \in AT_T$ then $[\xi\vartheta]^6 \in AT_{IAV}$.

G7. If $\xi \in AT_{IV/S}$ and $\vartheta \in AT_S$ then $[\xi\vartheta]^7 \in AT_{IV}$.

G8. If $\xi \in AT_{IV//IV}$ and $\vartheta \in AT_{IV}$ then $[\xi\vartheta]^8 \in AT_{IV}$.

G9. If $\xi \in AT_{S/S}$ and $\vartheta \in AT_S$ then $[\xi\vartheta]^9 \in AT_S$.

G10. If $\xi \in AT_{IV/IV}$ and $\vartheta \in AT_{IV}$ then $[\xi\vartheta]^{10} \in AT_{IV}$.

Rules of conjunction and disjunction

G11. If $\xi, \vartheta \in AT_S$ then $[\xi\vartheta]^{11a}, [\xi\vartheta]^{11b} \in AT_S$.

G12. If $\xi, \vartheta \in AT_{IV}$ then $[\xi\vartheta]^{12a}, [\xi\vartheta]^{12b} \in AT_{IV}$.

G13. If $\xi, \vartheta \in AT_T$ then $[\xi\vartheta]^{13} \in AT_T$.

Quantification rules. For each natural number n:

G14. If $\xi \in AT_T$ and $\vartheta \in AT_S$ then $[\xi\vartheta]^{14,n} \in AT_S$.

G15. If $\xi \in AT_T$ and $\vartheta \in AT_{CN}$ then $[\xi\vartheta]^{15,n} \in AT_{CN}$.

G16. If $\xi \in AT_T$ and $\vartheta \in AT_{IV}$ then $[\xi\vartheta]^{16,n} \in AT_{IV}$.

Negation and tense rules

G17. If $\xi \in AT_T$ and $\vartheta \in AT_{IV}$ then $[\xi\vartheta]^{17a}, [\xi\vartheta]^{17b}, [\xi\vartheta]^{17c}, [\xi\vartheta]^{17d}, [\xi\vartheta]^{17e} \in AT_S$.

The definition produces numbered bracketings like

$$[[\text{every man}]^3 [\text{love } [\text{a woman}]^3]^5]^4$$

and
$$[[\text{a woman}]^3[[\text{every man}]^3[\text{love he}_0]^5]^4]^{14,0}$$
(both elements of AT_S) and these bracketings dully keep track of the basic expressions that were used in order to form them and the rules by which these were combined. Here are more tree-like representations of the two analysis trees just given. Each non-terminal node is labeled with the number of the rule that led to the formation of the corresponding subtree.

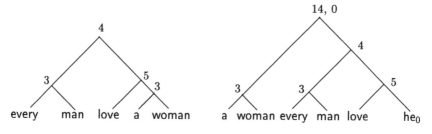

Syntax of the Fragment

Although our main interest lies in the semantic interpretation of analysis trees, we must of course assign expressions of English to them.[2] This we shall do by way of an inductive definition, letting the expression that is to be assigned to a complex tree be a function of the expressions that are assigned to its parts. The functions that we shall use are Montague's operations F_3–F_{15}, which are given below.

Definition 24 (Syntactic operations) Let γ and δ be strings. Define:

$F_{3,n}(\gamma, \delta) = \gamma$ such that δ'; and δ' comes from δ by replacing each occurrence of he$_n$ or him$_n$ by he/she/it or him/her/it respectively, according as the first B_{CN} in γ is of masc./fem./neuter gender.

$F_4(\gamma, \delta) = \gamma\delta'$, and δ' is the result of replacing the main verbs in δ by their third person singular present.

$F_5(\gamma, \delta) = \gamma\delta$ if δ does not have the form he$_n$ and $F_5(\gamma, \text{he}_n) = \text{him}_n$.

$F_6(\gamma, \delta) = F_7(\delta, \gamma) = \gamma\delta$.

$F_8(\gamma, \delta) = \gamma$ and δ; $F_9(\gamma, \delta) = \gamma$ or δ .

$F_{10,n}(\gamma, \delta)$ comes from δ by replacing the first occurrence of he$_n$ or him$_n$ by γ and all other occurrences of he$_n$ or him$_n$ by he/she/it or him/her/it respectively, according as the first B_{CN} or B_T in γ is

---

[2]Montague's syntax is awkward and is not the reason for studying Montague Grammar. Fortunately his semantics can be coupled to much less naive syntactic theories, as is shown for example in Generalized Phrase Structure Grammar and in modern versions of Categorial Grammar. For an interesting connection with Chomsky's Government and Binding framework see Bittner 1994. Here we shall be satisfied with presenting a variant of Montague's original syntax.

g	$S(g)$	g	$S(g)$	g	$S(g)$	g	$S(g)$
2, n	3, n	8	6	12b	9	17b	12
3	6	9	6	13	9	17c	13
4	4	10	7	14, n	10, n	17d	14
5	5	11a	8	15, n	10, n	17e	15
6	5	11b	9	16, n	10, n		
7	6	12a	8	17a	11		

TABLE 2

masc./fem./neuter, if γ does not have the form he_k and $F_{10,n}(he_k, \delta)$ comes from δ by replacing all occurrences of he_n or him_n by he_k or him_k respectively.

$F_{11}(\gamma, \delta) = \gamma\delta'$ and δ' is the result of replacing the first verb in δ by its negative third person singular present.

$F_{12}(\gamma, \delta) = \gamma\delta''$ and δ'' is the result of replacing the first verb in δ by its third person singular future.

$F_{13}(\gamma, \delta) = \gamma\delta'''$ and δ''' is the result of replacing the first verb in δ by its negative third person singular future.

$F_{14}(\gamma, \delta) = \gamma\delta''''$ and δ'''' is the result of replacing the first verb in δ by its third person singular present perfect.

$F_{15}(\gamma, \delta) = \gamma\delta'''''$ and δ''''' is the result of replacing the first verb in δ by its negative third person singular present perfect.

Using these functions we can give a compositional assignment of phrases to trees. The main thing is to stipulate which operation is used in which case.

Definition 25 (Phrases) For each analysis tree ξ, define a *phrase* $\sigma(\xi)$ by induction on the complexity of analysis trees:

S1. $\sigma(\xi) = \xi$ if $\xi \in B_A$

S2–S17. If g is a rule number and $S(g)$ is as in Table 2, then $\sigma([\xi\vartheta]^g) = F_{S(g)}(\sigma(\xi), \sigma(\vartheta))$.

By way of example I shall derive the phrases that are associated with the example trees that were given before. The first of these derivations proceeds as follows.

$$\sigma([[\text{every man}]^3[\text{love [a woman}]^3]^5]^4) =$$
$$F_4(F_6(\text{every, man}), F_5(\text{love}, F_6(\text{a, woman}))) =$$
$$F_4(\text{every man, love a woman}) =$$
$$\text{every man loves a woman}$$

The second derivation couples our second analysis tree to the same sentence:

$$\sigma([[\text{a woman}]^3[[\text{every man}]^3[\text{love he}_0]^5]^4]^{14,0}) \ =$$
$$F_{10,0}(F_6(\text{a, woman}), F_4(F_6(\text{every, man}), F_5(\text{love, he}_0))) \ =$$
$$F_{10,0}(\text{a woman}, F_4(\text{every man, love him}_0)) \ =$$
$$F_{10,0}(\text{a woman, every man loves him}_0) \ =$$
$$\text{every man loves a woman}$$

This means that the function σ is not one-one; the same phrase may be associated with different trees. The trees, on the other hand, are uniquely readable, as is trivial to see from their construction. We say that an analysis tree ξ is a *reading for* $\sigma(\xi)$ and conclude that a phrase may have different readings.

The present way of defining the syntax of the PTQ fragment differs somewhat from Montague's original set-up. Where we have defined analysis trees first and have assigned expressions of English to them inductively, Montague defines the latter directly and uses his analysis trees[3] only as a way to sum up their construction process. The technical gain of our approach is that we are now in the possession of a reasonably manageable unambiguous language of analysis trees that we can use to assign meanings to. In fact our approach conforms to the general program Montague set out in 'Universal Grammar' (Montague 1970) where ambiguous languages are interpreted through the mediation of 'disambiguated' languages. In his PTQ article, Montague himself deviated from this program.

But the advantage is not only technical, there is also a gain on a broader linguistic level. The separation of the syntactical operations of the language (F_3–F_{15} in the present case) from its grammatical rules (G1–G17 here) makes a rather nice distinction between those parts of the grammar that are language-dependent and those that are not. While Definition 23 could be used in setting up a fragment of any language, be it English, Dutch or Swahili, Definitions 22 and 24 are of course highly particular to the English tongue. Dowty 1982 has an interesting discussion of this point and traces the idea of separating grammatical rules and syntactic operations back to Curry 1963, who calls the universal part of language 'tectogrammatics', the language-particular part 'phenogrammatics'. Grammatical relations, like 'subject', 'object' and 'indirect object', are universal, and hence tectogrammatical, in nature, Dowty claims. And indeed it is easy to define such relations on the basis of our analysis trees. For more motivation along these lines see Dowty's work.

---

[3]Montague's analysis trees are just like ours, but are in a tree-like representation and have each node decorated by the prase that is assigned to the tree under that node.

Semantics of the Fragment

Let us turn to the semantics of the fragment. Wishing to formalize the way in which meanings are attached to expressions of English, we shall give a translation function $°$ sending analysis trees to terms of our relational logic TT_2. Since the terms of our logic are interpreted model-theoretically and since the translation will be well behaved, we may think of these translations as standing proxy for *meanings*. Each phrase Φ will be associated with a set of meanings $\{\xi° \mid \sigma(\xi) = \Phi\}$.

Analysis trees of a category A will be sent to terms of a fixed type that can be obtained from A using the following rule:

Definition 26 (Category-to-type Rule)[4]

   i. $\tau(E) = e$; $\tau(S) = \langle s \rangle$;
   ii. $\tau(A/B) = \tau(A//B) = \tau(B) * \tau(A)$,
      where $\beta * \langle \alpha_1 \ldots \alpha_n \rangle = \langle \beta \alpha_1 \ldots \alpha_n \rangle$ for all β, α_1, $\ldots$, α_n.

The idea is that the meaning of a sentence is a proposition (a type $\langle s \rangle$ object, a set of indices), that the meaning of an expression of category E (these do not actually occur in the fragment) is a possible individual and that the meaning of an expression of any category expecting a B in order to form an A has a type that expects a $\tau(B)$ to form a $\tau(A)$. Note that, contrary to what is usual,[5] the translation of an expression will be its meaning, its intension, not its extension. Of course, the extension of an expression at any index can always be obtained from its intension.

In Table 3 the values of the function τ are written out for those categories that are actually used in the PTQ fragment. In the third column we give the IL types that are assigned to these categories in DWP for comparison.

To see that objects of type $\tau(A)$ are indeed the kind of objects one would like to assign to expressions of category A we may use the slice functions discussed previously. For example, one would arguably like the intension of a CN or an IV to be a property (of individuals), a function from possible worlds to sets of entities. The second slice function of any type $\langle es \rangle$ object is just this kind of thing. In a similar way we see that the meaning of a term is a property of properties (a quantifier), a function

---

[4]Lewis 1974 gives the following category-to-type rule (using functional types of course):

   i. $\tau_L(E) = se$; $\tau_L(S) = st$;
   ii. $\tau_L(A/B) = \tau_L(A//B) = (\tau_L(B)\tau_L(A))$

Adopting Bennett's Simplification one obtains the following rule:

   i. $\tau'(E) = e$; $\tau'(S) = st$;
   ii. $\tau'(A/B) = \tau'(A//B) = (\tau'(B)\tau'(A))$

Our rule is equivalent to this last one in the sense that $\tau'(A) = \Sigma(\tau(A))$, where the function Σ is as in Chapter 2.

[5]See however Lewis 1974 and Thomason's Introduction to Montague 1974.

Category A	$\tau(A)$	$f(A)$
S	$\langle s \rangle$	t
S/E	$\langle es \rangle$	et
$S//E$	$\langle es \rangle$	et
S/S	$\langle\langle s\rangle s\rangle$	$(st)t$
S/IV	$\langle\langle es\rangle s\rangle$	$(s(et))t$
IV/S	$\langle\langle s\rangle es\rangle$	$(st)(et)$
IV/IV	$\langle\langle es\rangle es\rangle$	$(s(et))(et)$
$IV//IV$	$\langle\langle es\rangle es\rangle$	$(s(et))(et)$
IV/T	$\langle\langle\langle es\rangle s\rangle es\rangle$	$(s((s(et))t))(et)$
DET	$\langle\langle es\rangle\langle es\rangle s\rangle$	$(s(et))((s(et))t)$
IAV/T	$\langle\langle\langle es\rangle s\rangle\langle es\rangle es\rangle$	$(s((s(et))t))((s(et))(et))$

TABLE 3

from possible worlds to sets of properties; the meaning of an IV/IV is a function from properties to properties, and so on. The intension of a determiner can either be seen as a function from properties to quantifiers (use the first slice function) or as a so-called relation-in-intension between properties, a function from possible worlds to relations between properties (use the third slice function). Both perspectives have been advocated in the literature.

We now can translate each expression of the fragment into type theory inductively, by giving translations to all lexical items and by telling how the translation of a complex expression is to depend on the translations of its parts.

Constants	Type
john, bill, mary	e
run, walk, talk	$\langle es \rangle$
man, woman, park, fish, pen, unicorn	$\langle es \rangle$
believe, assert	$\langle\langle s\rangle es\rangle$
find, lose, eat, love, date	$\langle ees \rangle$
seek, conceive	$\langle\langle\langle es\rangle s\rangle es\rangle$
rapidly, slowly, voluntarily, allegedly	$\langle\langle es\rangle es\rangle$
try, wish	$\langle\langle es\rangle es\rangle$
in	$\langle\langle\langle es\rangle s\rangle\langle es\rangle es\rangle$
about	$\langle e\langle es\rangle es\rangle$
$<, \approx$	$\langle ss \rangle$

TABLE 4

Definition 27 (Translation) Let the constants in the first column of Table 4 have types as indicated in the second column. For each analysis tree ξ define its translation $\xi°$ by induction on the complexity of analysis trees:

Basic rule

T1. $\quad$ run$°$ = *run*, walk$°$ = *walk*, talk$°$ = *talk*;
$\quad$ John$°$ = $\lambda P\,(Pjohn)$, Mary$°$ = $\lambda P\,(Pmary)$,
$\quad$ Bill$°$ = $\lambda P\,(Pbill)$, he$_n°$ = $\lambda P\,(Px_n)$;
$\quad$ believe that$°$ = *believe*, assert that$°$ = *assert*
$\quad$ find$°$ = $\lambda Q\lambda y(Q\lambda x(find\ xy))$, lose$°$ = $\lambda Q\lambda y(Q\lambda x(lose\ xy))$,
$\quad$ eat$°$ = $\lambda Q\lambda y(Q\lambda x(eat\ xy))$, love$°$ = $\lambda Q\lambda y(Q\lambda x(love\ xy))$,
$\quad$ date$°$ = $\lambda Q\lambda y(Q\lambda x(date\ xy))$, be$°$ = $\lambda Q\lambda y(Q\lambda x\lambda i(x = y))$,
$\quad$ seek$°$ = *seek*, conceive$°$ = *conceive*
$\quad$ rapidly$°$ = *rapidly* , slowly$°$ = *slowly*
$\quad$ voluntarily$°$ = *voluntarily*, allegedly$°$ = *allegedly*;
$\quad$ try to$°$ = *try*, wish to$°$ = *wish*;
$\quad$ man$°$ = *man*, woman$°$ = *woman* park$°$ = *park*,
$\quad$ fish$°$ = *fish*, pen$°$ = *pen*, unicorn$°$ = *unicorn*;
$\quad$ every$°$ = $\lambda P_1\lambda P_2\lambda i\forall x\,(P_1xi \rightarrow P_2xi)$,
$\quad$ a$°$ = $\lambda P_1\lambda P_2\lambda i\exists x\,(P_1xi \wedge P_2xi)$,
$\quad$ the$°$ = $\lambda P_1\lambda P_2\lambda i\exists x\,(\forall y\,(P_1yi \leftrightarrow x = y) \wedge P_2xi)$;
$\quad$ necessarily$°$ = $\lambda p\lambda i\forall j\,(pj)$;
$\quad$ in$°$ = $\lambda Q\lambda P\lambda y(Q\lambda x\,(in\ xPy))$, about$°$ = *about*

Relative clause rule. For each natural number n:

T2. $\qquad ([\xi\vartheta]^{2,n})° = \lambda x_n\lambda i\,(\xi°x_ni \wedge \vartheta°i)$;

Rules of functional application.

T3–T10. $([\xi\vartheta]^k)° = \xi°\vartheta°$ if $3 \le k \le 10$;

Rules of conjunction and disjunction.

T11. $\qquad ([\xi\vartheta]^{11a})° = \lambda i\,(\xi°i \wedge \vartheta°i)$;
$\qquad ([\xi\vartheta]^{11b})° = \lambda i\,(\xi°i \vee \vartheta°i)$;
T12. $\qquad ([\xi\vartheta]^{12a})° = \lambda x\lambda i\,(\xi°xi \wedge \vartheta°xi)$;
$\qquad ([\xi\vartheta]^{12b})° = \lambda x\lambda i\,(\xi°xi \vee \vartheta°xi)$;
T13. $\qquad ([\xi\vartheta]^{13})° = \lambda P\lambda i(\xi°Pi \vee \vartheta°Pi)$;

Quantification rules. For each natural number n:

T14. $\qquad ([\xi\vartheta]^{14,n})° = \xi°\lambda x_n\,(\vartheta°)$;
T15. $\qquad ([\xi\vartheta]^{15,n})° = \lambda y(\xi°\lambda x_n\,(\vartheta°y))$;
T16. $\qquad ([\xi\vartheta]^{16,n})° = \lambda y\,(\xi°\lambda x_n\,(\vartheta°y))$;

Negation and tense rules.

T17. $\qquad ([\xi\vartheta]^{17a})° = \lambda i\neg\xi°\vartheta°i$;
$\qquad ([\xi\vartheta]^{17b})° = \lambda i\exists j\,(i < j \wedge i \approx j \wedge \xi°\vartheta°j)$;

$$([\xi\vartheta]^{17c})^\circ = \lambda i \neg \exists j \, (i < j \land i \approx j \land \xi^\circ \vartheta^\circ j);$$
$$([\xi\vartheta]^{17d})^\circ = \lambda i \exists j \, (j < i \land i \approx j \land \xi^\circ \vartheta^\circ j);$$
$$([\xi\vartheta]^{17e})^\circ = \lambda i \neg \exists j \, (j < i \land i \approx j \land \xi^\circ \vartheta^\circ j).$$

In the above definition and in the rest of the book we let x, y and z range over individuals (type e), i and j over indices (type s), p and q over propositions (type $\langle s \rangle$), P over properties (type $\langle es \rangle$) and Q over quantifiers (type $\langle\langle es\rangle s\rangle$). In order to show how the definition works, we shall translate our two example trees into type logic. The first translation proceeds as follows.

1. $\mathsf{a}^\circ = \lambda P_1 \lambda P_2 \lambda i \exists x \, (P_1 xi \land P_2 xi)$
2. $\mathsf{woman}^\circ = woman$
3. $([\mathsf{a\ woman}]^3)^\circ = \lambda P_1 \lambda P_2 \lambda i \exists x \, (P_1 xi \land P_2 xi) woman \rightsquigarrow$
   $\lambda P \lambda i \exists x \, (woman \, xi \land Pxi)$
4. $\mathsf{love}^\circ = \lambda Q \lambda y (Q \lambda x (love \, xy))$
5. $([\mathsf{love[a\ woman]}^3]^5)^\circ \rightsquigarrow$
   $\lambda Q \lambda y (Q \lambda x (love \, xy)) \lambda P \lambda i \exists x \, (woman \, xi \land Pxi) \rightsquigarrow$
   $\lambda y (\lambda P \lambda i \exists x \, (woman \, xi \land Pxi) \lambda x (love \, xy)) \rightsquigarrow$
   $\lambda y \lambda i \exists x \, (woman \, xi \land \lambda x \, (love \, xy) xi)) \rightsquigarrow$
   $\lambda y \lambda i \exists x \, (woman \, xi \land love \, xyi)$
6. $\mathsf{every}^\circ = \lambda P_1 \lambda P_2 \lambda i \forall x \, (P_1 xi \rightarrow P_2 xi)$
7. $\mathsf{man}^\circ = man$
8. $([\mathsf{every\ man}]^3)^\circ = \lambda P_1 \lambda P_2 \lambda i \forall x \, (P_1 xi \rightarrow P_2 xi) man \rightsquigarrow$
   $\lambda P \lambda i \forall x \, (man \, xi \rightarrow Pxi)$
9. $([[\mathsf{every\ man}]^3 [\mathsf{love[a\ woman]}^3]^5]^4)^\circ \rightsquigarrow$
   $\lambda P \lambda i \forall x \, (man \, xi \rightarrow Pxi) \lambda y \lambda i \exists x \, (woman \, xi \land love xyi)) \rightsquigarrow$
   $\lambda i \forall x \, (man \, xi \rightarrow \lambda y \lambda i \exists x \, (woman \, xi \land love \, xyi)) xi) \rightsquigarrow$
   $\lambda i \forall x \, (man xi \rightarrow \lambda y \lambda i \exists z \, (woman \, zi \land love \, zyi)) xi) \rightsquigarrow$
   $\lambda i \forall x \, (man \, xi \rightarrow \exists z \, (woman \, zi \land love \, zxi))$

Here is the translation of our second example tree.

1. $\mathsf{love}^\circ = \lambda Q \lambda y \, (Q \lambda x \, (love \, xy))$
2. $\mathsf{he}_0^\circ = \lambda P (Px_0)$
3. $([\mathsf{love\ he}_0]^5)^\circ = \lambda Q \lambda y (Q \lambda x \, (love \, xy)) \lambda P (Px_0) \rightsquigarrow$
   $\lambda y (\lambda P (Px_0) \lambda x (love \, xy)) \rightsquigarrow$
   $\lambda y (\lambda x (love \, xy) x_0) \rightsquigarrow$
   $\lambda y (love \, x_0 y) \rightsquigarrow$
   $love \, x_0$
4. $([\mathsf{every\ man}]^3)^\circ \rightsquigarrow$
   $\lambda P \lambda i \forall x \, (man \, xi \rightarrow Pxi)$
5. $([[\mathsf{every\ man}]^3 [\mathsf{love\ he}_0]^5]^4)^\circ \rightsquigarrow$

$\lambda P \lambda i \forall x \, (man \ xi \rightarrow Pxi) love \ x_0 \rightsquigarrow$

$\lambda i \forall x \, (manxi \rightarrow love \ x_0 xi)$

6. $([a \ woman]^3)^\circ \rightsquigarrow$

$\lambda P \lambda i \exists x \, (woman \ xi \wedge Pxi)$

7. $([[a \ woman]^3 [[every \ man]^3 [love \ he_0]^5]^4]^{14,0})^\circ \rightsquigarrow$

$\lambda P \lambda i \exists x \, (woman \ xi \wedge Pxi) \lambda x_0 \lambda i \forall x \, (man \ xi \rightarrow love \ x_0 xi) \rightsquigarrow$

$\lambda P \lambda i \exists y \, (woman \ yi \wedge Pyi) \lambda x_0 \lambda i \forall x \, (man \ xi \rightarrow love \ x_0 xi) \rightsquigarrow$

$\lambda i \exists y \, (woman \ yi \wedge \lambda x_0 \lambda i \forall x \, (man \ xi \rightarrow love \ x_0 xi) yi) \rightsquigarrow$

$\lambda i \exists y \, (woman \ yi \wedge \forall x \, (man \ xi \rightarrow love \ yxi))$

Entailment

Let us give a precise definition of the notion of logical consequence on our natural language fragment. Using the somewhat generalized form of the definition of TT_2 entailment given in Chapter 2, we can define the relation as a relation in all categories; we need not restrict it to sentences. If Γ and Δ are sets of terms of type $\langle \alpha_1 \ldots \alpha_n \rangle$, we write $\Gamma \models_{AX} \Delta$ for

$$\Gamma, \{\lambda x_{\alpha_1} \ldots \lambda x_{\alpha_n} \varphi \mid \varphi \in AX\} \models_s \Delta,$$

where AX is the set $\{AX1, \ldots, AX8\}$. We say that an analysis tree ϑ of any category *follows from* a set of trees Ξ of the same category if and only if it holds that $\Xi^\circ \models_{AX} \vartheta^\circ$. For analysis trees of sentence category S (that have translations of type $\langle s \rangle$) this amounts to stipulating that (in each model in which indices behave like world-time pairs) at each index at which all propositions expressed by the premises are true the proposition expressed by the conclusion is true.

This entailment relation is equivalent to the one given in DWP. The following theorem states this; its proof and more precise information about the translation function $'$ and set of IL sentences Δ that it mentions are given in the Appendix.

Theorem 3 *For each analysis tree ξ let ξ' be the translation it is given in DWP. Let Δ be a set of DWP meaning postulates, to be specified in the Appendix, and let $\Xi \cup \{\vartheta\}$ be a set of analysis trees, then:*

$$\Xi^\circ \models_{AX} \vartheta^\circ \ in \ TT_2 \quad iff \quad \Xi', \Delta \models \vartheta' \ in \ IL.$$

5

Going Partial I: Propositional Logic and Predicate Logic

One of the basic assumptions of classical logic is the assumption that a sentence is false if and only if it is not true. Very often the word 'false' is even taken to be just an abbreviation of the words 'not true'. Thus two possibilities are excluded:

(a)   that sentences are neither true nor false;
(b)   that sentences are both true and false.

Partial logics are logics in which at least one of these possibilities is allowed. In this chapter we shall develop partial variants of classical propositional logic and classical predicate logic. In the next chapter we shall generalize these to a full partial theory of types.

Should we allow both (a) and (b) or will it do to allow just (a) or just (b)? Between the last two possibilities there is not much to choose, since under certain reasonable assumptions a logic that allows sentences to be both true and false but does not allow them to be neither will be isomorphic to a logic that does the reverse. But the choice between a logic that allows all four possible combinations of truth values and one that allows only three of them is real.

I shall allow both overdefinedness and underdefinedness here. For this I have two reasons. The first one is of a purely formal, aesthetic nature: accepting one, but not the other, of the two symmetrical possibilities (a) and (b) above would introduce certain asymmetries into the logic that are less than nice. Four-valued logics tend to be more elegant than three-valued ones. My second reason derives from one of the applications I intend the logic to be used for: It seems that if we want to give a natural account of the semantics of the psychological verbs, we need situations that are overdefined as well as situations that are underdefined. Good examples of underdefined situations are people's visual scenes, the situations they see at some given moment. Examples of overdefined situations must necessarily have a less concrete character: since reality is coherent, no overdefined situation can be part of reality in the way a visual scene is part of it.[1] But people do not only see things, they imagine and believe things as well. And this is where incoherence gets in, since imagined situations can be incoherent. People can believe things to be and not to be the case, or at least they can believe that they believe this. It is therefore useful to have overdefined situations around if you want to model the logic of the verbs believe, imagine, dream and the like. As long as we remember that incoherent situations cannot of course have any claim to concreteness, it seems legitimate to use them in semantics.

I realize that not all readers will like my decision to allow overdefinedness as well as its opposite. Fortunately, however, the logic that is to be developed below is very easily adapted to a three-valued one. Those who prefer to exclude overdefinedness will have no difficulty in making the minimal changes that are needed to do this. These readers will also find that many of the applications of the four-valued logic in the next chapters will carry over to their three-valued variant without any problems.

Now that the tie between truth and falsity has been cut, we are left with four combinations of truth values: 'true and not false', 'false and not true', 'neither true nor false' and 'both true and false'. Following Belnap 1977 I abbreviate these combinations as $\mathbf{T}$, $\mathbf{F}$, $\mathbf{N}$ and $\mathbf{B}$ respectively and I shall say that a combination $\mathbf{X}$ *includes truth* iff $\mathbf{X}$ equals $\mathbf{T}$ or $\mathbf{B}$ and that $\mathbf{X}$ *includes falsity* iff $\mathbf{X}$ equals $\mathbf{F}$ or $\mathbf{B}$.[2] Note that $\mathbf{T}$, $\mathbf{F}$, $\mathbf{N}$ and $\mathbf{B}$ are not truth values themselves, they are *truth combinations*. Conceptually this makes an important difference. Nevertheless, conforming to usual practice we shall call logics that allow all combinations of truth values *four-valued*, those that allow only $\mathbf{T}$, $\mathbf{F}$ and $\mathbf{N}$ *three-valued*.

---

[1] The sentences we usually encounter in Montague Grammar, sentences not containing truth predicates etc., are always either true or false and never both in the real world (but they may be neither true nor false in parts of the real world or both true and false in imagined situations). In the next chapter we shall make sure that this is the case in all models under consideration by means of a meaning postulate. Of course the situation may be different with respect to the Liar sentence, which is treated as neither true nor false or as both true and false in most contemporary theories. Although the logic that is developed below is a higher order generalization of the four-valued predicate logic that is usually employed in analyses of the Liar paradox (see Woodruff 1984, Visser 1984), we postpone a treatment of the Liar within the present framework to another occasion.

[2] $\mathbf{T}$, $\mathbf{F}$, $\mathbf{N}$ and $\mathbf{B}$ are often defined as $\{true\}$, $\{false\}$, $\emptyset$ and $\{true, false\}$ respectively. A truth combination $\mathbf{X}$ can then be said to include truth (falsity) if $true \in \mathbf{X}$ ($false \in \mathbf{X}$). This is elegant but I shall not adopt this definition for the reason that union and intersection on these sets do not correspond to disjunction and conjunction respectively. (They do however correspond to the operations $\sqcup$ and $\sqcap$ to be defined below.)

Partial Propositional Logic

How does the truth combination of a complex sentence depend on the truth combinations of its parts? A stunningly simple answer to this question (for the sentences of classical propositional logic) was given by Dunn 1976. Truth and falsity can be computed just as it is done ordinarily, provided that truth conditions and falsity conditions are separated:

i. $\neg\varphi$ is true if and only if φ is false,
   $\neg\varphi$ is false if and only if φ is true;

ii. $\varphi \wedge \psi$ is true if and only if φ is true and ψ is true,
   $\varphi \wedge \psi$ is false if and only if φ is false or ψ is false;

iii. $\varphi \vee \psi$ is true if and only if φ is true or ψ is true,
   $\varphi \vee \psi$ is false if and only if φ is false and ψ is false.

So, for example, if φ receives the combination **N** and ψ gets the combination **T**, then $\varphi \wedge \psi$ gets **N**: $\varphi \wedge \psi$ is not true since φ isn't and it is not false since neither φ nor ψ is. Reasoning similarly in all other cases we obtain the following tables for the classical connectives:

$\wedge$	**T**	**F**	**N**	**B**		$\vee$	**T**	**F**	**N**	**B**		$\neg$	
T	**T**	**F**	**N**	**B**		**T**	**T**	**T**	**T**	**T**		**T**	**F**
F	**F**	**F**	**F**	**F**		**F**	**T**	**F**	**N**	**B**		**F**	**T**
N	**N**	**F**	**N**	**F**		**N**	**T**	**N**	**N**	**T**		**N**	**N**
B	**B**	**F**	**F**	**B**		**B**	**T**	**B**	**T**	**B**		**B**	**B**

Note that if we restrict these tables to $\{\mathbf{T}, \mathbf{F}, \mathbf{N}\}$ we obtain just the Strong Kleene tables; following Visser 1984 we shall therefore call the above the *Extended Strong Kleene* tables. The two-place function on $\{\mathbf{T}, \mathbf{F}, \mathbf{N}, \mathbf{B}\}$ given by the table for conjunction will be denoted by $\cap$ and similarly $\cup$ will denote the function given by the table for disjunction; the one-place function given by the negation table we shall denote with $-$. We write $\mathbf{X} \sqsubseteq \mathbf{Y}$ iff for some $\mathbf{Z}$, $\mathbf{X} \cup \mathbf{Z}$ equals $\mathbf{Y}$. Notice that $\mathbf{X} \sqsubseteq \mathbf{Y}$ if and only if $\mathbf{Y}$ includes truth if $\mathbf{X}$ does and $\mathbf{X}$ includes falsity if $\mathbf{Y}$ includes falsity. The partial order $\sqsubseteq$, a generalization of the ordering relation in the Boolean algebra $\{true, false\}$, will play the role of *entailment* in the logics to be defined below.

The operations $\cap$ and $\cup$ form a distributive lattice on the set of truth combinations. This lattice is depicted with the help of a Hasse diagram as L4 below (L4 is discussed extensively in Belnap 1977).

Adding negation to L4 (note that this operation corresponds with rotating L4 halfway around its **B-N** axis) gives a structure that conforms to almost all of the customary axioms of the theory of Boolean algebra's.

To be more precise, the structure LK4 = $\langle \{\mathbf{T}, \mathbf{F}, \mathbf{N}, \mathbf{B}\}, \cap, \cup, -, \mathbf{T}, \mathbf{F} \rangle$ satisfies the following list of axioms:

   i. The axioms for distributive lattices;

   ii. $0 + a = a$, $1 \cdot a = a$;

   iii. $a'' = a$;

   iv. $(a \cdot b)' = a' + b'$, $(a + b)' = a' \cdot b'$,

   v. $0' = 1$, $1' = 0$.

Any structure that obeys this list of axioms I shall call a *Kleene algebra*.

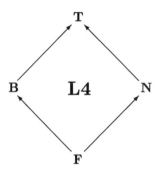

Logical lattice

There are two Boolean axioms that do not hold in LK4 and that, of course, we don't want to hold: $a + a' = 1$ and $a \cdot a' = 0$. If we would add them to the above list of axioms we would get a full set of axioms for Boolean algebras. So the algebra of truth combinations differs only minimally from the algebra of truth values; the move from single truth values to combinations of them did not cause an unmotivated loss of algebraical properties.

There is a Kleene algebra different from LK4 on the set $\{\mathbf{T}, \mathbf{F}, \mathbf{N}, \mathbf{B}\}$ that deserves our interest. Let us say that a truth combination $\mathbf{X}$ *approximates* a truth combination $\mathbf{Y}$, $\mathbf{X} \sqsubseteq \mathbf{Y}$, if and only if $\mathbf{Y}$ includes truth if $\mathbf{X}$ does and $\mathbf{Y}$ includes falsity if $\mathbf{X}$ includes falsity. Intuitively, if $\mathbf{X} \sqsubseteq \mathbf{Y}$ then $\mathbf{Y}$ contains at least as much information as $\mathbf{X}$ does. The relation $\sqsubseteq$ on the truth combinations gives rise to the distributive lattice A4 below. Clearly, A4 is just L4 put on its side. Its meet and join correspond to two natural ways to combine information. If one good friend tells you that a certain rumour is true and another equally good friend tells you that it is false, there are two evenhanded ways to combine the information that they have given you. One would be to accept that the rumour is both true and false, another would be that it is neither. Note that the meet of two truth combinations $\mathbf{X}$ and $\mathbf{Y}$ in A4, written $\mathbf{X} \sqcap \mathbf{Y}$, includes truth (falsity) iff both **X** and **Y** include truth (falsity). The join **X** ⊔ **Y**, includes truth (falsity) iff either **X** or **Y** includes truth (falsity).

These join and meet operations are what we can call *half-duals* of the operations ⊔ and ⊓ defined above and we can also define a half-dual of negation: this is the unary operation ⌐ that leaves **T** and **F** fixed, but swaps **B** and **N**. That is, ⌐**X** includes truth (falsity) iff **X** does not include falsity (truth). The structure ⟨{**T**, **F**, **N**, **B**}, ⊓, ⊔, ⌐, **B**, **N**⟩, which we shall call AK4, is a Kleene algebra.

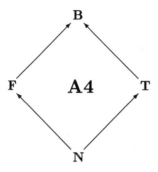

Approximation lattice

At this point we may introduce propositional connectives corresponding to our new operations on truth combinations. Let us write ⊗, ⊕ and ⌐ for the connectives that are to be interpreted as ⊓, ⊔ and ⌐ respectively (so ⌐ does double duty as a sign to denote a connective and as a sign to denote its interpretation). Then these connectives get the following truth tables.

⊗	**T**	**F**	**N**	**B**		⊕	**T**	**F**	**N**	**B**		⌐	
T	**T**	**N**	**N**	**T**		**T**	**T**	**B**	**T**	**B**		**T**	**T**
F	**N**	**F**	**N**	**F**		**F**	**B**	**F**	**F**	**B**		**F**	**F**
N	**N**	**N**	**N**	**N**		**N**	**T**	**F**	**N**	**B**		**N**	**B**
B	**T**	**F**	**N**	**B**		**B**	**B**	**B**	**B**	**B**		**B**	**N**

The connective ⊗ is what Blamey 1986 calls *interjunction*. It has the truth conditions of ∧ but the falsity conditions of ∨, while its dual ⊕ has the truth conditions of ∨ and the falsity conditions of ∧. We see here that our decision to severe the classical connection between truth and falsity does not only lead to a strengthening of the entailment relation, it also leads to a complete set of half-duals of our ordinary logical concepts. As entailment corresponds to the L4 ordering while approximation is the A4 ordering, we can even say that approximation is the half-dual of entailment.

Elementary considerations[3] show that the new connectives $\otimes$, $\oplus$ and $\lrcorner$ are not definable in terms of their classical half-duals $\wedge$, $\vee$ and $\neg$; and this is an important reason to allow for these strange new symbols. After all, the importance of the classical connectives largely derives from the fact that these are *expressively adequate* for classical logic—every truth function can be expressed using them. In a logic where this property is lost there is no longer reason to restrict ourselves to the familiar connectives. As we shall see shortly the set $\{\otimes, \lrcorner, \wedge, \neg\}$ is adequate to express any function on the truth combinations.

In order to define a partial propositional logic we need to augment the syntax of ordinary two-valued propositional logic with new connectives and in the light of the previous remarks the reader will expect the addition of $\otimes$ and $\lrcorner$ to the set of connectives. I find it expedient, however, to choose another set of primitives. Apart from the classical $\wedge$ and $\neg$, these will be #, $\star$ and =, the first two of which are logical constants of formula type, intended to denote **B** and **N** respectively, and the third of which is a two-place connective denoting identity. (Notice that $\leftrightarrow$, if we give it its usual definition in terms of $\wedge$ and $\neg$, can no longer do duty as identity as it does in two-valued propositional logic, since $\varphi \leftrightarrow \psi$ gets the value **N** if both φ and ψ get the value **N**.) The choice of = as a primitive symbol rather than $\otimes$ and $\lrcorner$ is taken with a view to the generalization to the theory of types that we are after: in type theory we want to be able to express that objects of equal type are identical whatever this type is, so we shall need a symbol to express identity between objects of formula type $\langle\rangle$ anyhow.

Having augmented the syntax of propositional logic thus, we can now give a partial semantics.

Definition 28 (Tarski truth definition for partial propositional logic) Let L be a set of propositional constants and let $V : L \to \{\mathbf{T}, \mathbf{F}, \mathbf{N}, \mathbf{B}\}$ be a (*valuation*) *function*. The *value* $\|\varphi\|^V$ of a formula φ under V is defined as follows:

  i. $\|p\|^V = V(p)$ if $p \in L$;
  ii. $\|\neg\varphi\|^V = -\|\varphi\|^V$;
  $\|\varphi \wedge \psi\|^V = \|\varphi\|^V \cap \|\psi\|^V$;
  $\|\#\|^V = \mathbf{B}$;
  $\|\star\|^V = \mathbf{N}$;
  $\|\varphi = \psi\|^V = \mathbf{T}$ if $\|\varphi\|^V = \|\psi\|^V$
  $= \mathbf{F}$ if $\|\varphi\|^V \neq \|\psi\|^V$;

The clauses for negation, conjunction, # and $\star$ are clearly in agreement with the preceding discussion; the clause for = we shall discuss shortly. We

---

[3]Note that $\{\mathbf{T}, \mathbf{F}\}$ is closed under the classical operations, but not under $\sqcap$ or $\sqcup$, and that $\{\mathbf{T}, \mathbf{F}, \mathbf{N}\}$ is closed under the classical operations but not under $\lrcorner$.

can now define $\otimes$, $\oplus$ and $\sqcup$ and the classical abbreviatory symbols from the primitive connectives that we have chosen.

Definition 29 (Abbreviations) Write

$\top$	for[4]	$\star = \star$
$\bot$	for	$\neg \top$
$\varphi \vee \psi$	for	$\neg(\neg\varphi \wedge \neg\psi)$
$\varphi \rightarrow \psi$	for	$\neg\varphi \vee \psi$
$\varphi \leftrightarrow \psi$	for	$(\varphi \rightarrow \psi) \wedge (\psi \rightarrow \varphi)$
$\varphi @ \psi$	for	$(\varphi \wedge \#) \vee (\psi \wedge \star)$
$\varphi \otimes \psi$	for	$(\varphi \wedge \psi) @ (\varphi \vee \psi)$
$\varphi \oplus \phi$	for	$(\varphi \vee \psi) @ (\varphi \wedge \psi)$
$\sqcup\varphi$	for	$\neg(\varphi = \bot) \wedge$
		$((\varphi = \star) \rightarrow \#) \wedge ((\varphi = \#) \rightarrow \star)$

Notice that $\varphi @ \psi$ has the truth conditions of φ but the falsity conditions of ψ and hence the right operations are assigned to $\otimes$ and $\oplus$. More generally, under these definitions all connectives discussed above get the interpretation we want them to have.

Let us say that a valuation V *verifies* (*falsifies*) a formula φ if $\|\varphi\|^V$ includes truth (falsity). Letting $\bigcap$ and $\bigcup$ denote the infimum and the supremum of sets of truth combinations in the logical lattice L4, we define entailment thus:

Definition 30 (Entailment in partial propositional logic) Let Γ and Δ be sets of formulae. Γ *entails* Δ, $\Gamma \models \Delta$, if

$$\bigcap_{\varphi \in \Gamma} \|\varphi\|^V \subseteq \bigcup_{\psi \in \Delta} \|\psi\|^V$$

for all valuations V.

The resulting notion of logical consequence is double-barrelled: A set of premises entails a set of conclusions if and only if two conditions hold. The first of these is that each valuation that verifies all premises verifies some conclusion and the second is that each valuation that falsifies all conclusions falsifies some premise. This coincides with Blamey's 1986 definition and with the one given in Belnap 1977, who, like us, lets entailment go up hill in the logical lattice L4. Logical consequence is preservation of truth in one direction and preservation of falsity in the other.

There are two obvious single-barrelled alternatives to Definition 30. Write $\varphi \models' \psi$ iff each valuation that verifies φ verifies ψ, and write $\varphi \models'' \psi$ iff each valuation that falsifies ψ falsifies φ. Why did we not take either

---

[4]Warning: while $\top$ is often used to denote the top element of the approximation lattice A4, we follow the established practice to let it be the formula that is always true and never false, that is, it denotes the top of the logical lattice L4; a similar remark can be made with respect to the symbol $\bot$.

of these as our definition of entailment? The reason is that there are some important properties that $\models$ does, but that $\models'$ and $\models''$ do not, share with the classical notion of entailment. Blamey 1986 gives some examples. The first of these is Contraposition; we have:

$$\varphi \models \psi \text{ if and only if } \neg\psi \models \neg\varphi.$$

On the other hand neither $\models'$ nor $\models''$ satisfies this property. We have for example that $\star \models' \perp$ but not that $\neg\perp \models' \neg\star$. A second desirable property that our entailment notion has but that the other two lack is the following natural relation to the notion of logical equivalence:

$$\varphi \cong \psi \text{ if and only if } \varphi \models \psi \text{ and } \psi \models \varphi.$$

Here $\varphi \cong \psi$ (φ and ψ are logically equivalent) is defined by: $\|\varphi\|^V = \|\psi\|^V$ for each valuation V. As regards to the competing notions, note for example that both $\star \models' \perp$ and $\perp \models' \star$, but of course $\star$ and $\perp$ get different values.

A third property that Blamey mentions is the following classical correspondence:

$$\varphi \models \psi \text{ if and only if } \varphi \cong \varphi \wedge \psi \text{ if and only if } \psi \cong \varphi \vee \psi.$$

Again this fails for the other relations; we have for example that $\star \models' \perp$ but not that $\star \cong \star \wedge \perp$.

We see here that an adoption of $\models'$ or of $\models''$ as our notion of logical consequence would lead to deviations from classical logic that are unaccounted for by our original motivation of cutting the tie between truth and falsity. All this is of course a consequence of the fact that $\models$ is defined on the basis of the ordering relation in the Kleene algebra LK4 while its competitors are not. We can however define $\models'$ and $\models''$ in terms of $\models$ since it holds that:

$$\varphi \models' \psi \text{ if and only if } \varphi \models \psi, \star$$
$$\varphi \models'' \psi \text{ if and only if } \varphi, \star \models \psi.$$

Note moreover that for φ, ψ that contain only the classical $\neg$, $\wedge$, $\top$ and $\perp$ and the identity connective $=$, the three entailment notions correspond: for such formulae it holds that $\varphi \models \psi$ iff $\varphi \models' \psi$ iff $\varphi \models'' \psi$.[5] The easy proof is left to the reader.

Having settled the matter of entailment we return to the discussion of the identity clause in Definition 28. This clause seems the only reasonable one once we are given the constraint that identity statements $\varphi = \psi$ are two-valued, that is, if they always get the value **T** or **F**. But what about this requirement? Aren't there reasonable definitions of the semantics of $=$ such that an identity formula $\varphi = \psi$ could in some cases get a value **N** or **B**?

---

[5]Michael Morreau drew my attention to this fact.

The answer is no. The possibility is ruled out by the requirement that identity should satisfy the identity axioms, that is, the demand that the following should hold:

$$\models \varphi = \varphi$$
$$\varphi = \psi, [\psi/p]\chi \models [\varphi/p]\chi.$$

Suppose that in Definition 28 we had adopted some alternative clause for $=$, but that the two statements above would still hold. We derive that even then no formula $\varphi = \psi$ would get $\mathbf{B}$ or $\mathbf{N}$ as a value under any valuation. From $\models \varphi = \varphi$ it follows that $\varphi = \varphi$ must always get the value $\mathbf{T}$ and hence that $\neg(\varphi = \varphi)$ must get the value $\mathbf{F}$. An instantiation of the other statement gives $\varphi = \psi, \neg(\varphi = \psi) \models \neg(\varphi = \varphi)$. From the assumption that $\|\varphi = \psi\|^V = \mathbf{N}$ for some V we derive $\mathbf{N} \subseteq \mathbf{F}$, which is absurd and from the assumption that $\|\varphi = \psi\|^V = \mathbf{B}$ we derive that $\mathbf{B} \subseteq \mathbf{F}$, no less absurd. We see that if $=$ is to satisfy the identity axioms it has to be two-valued.

We now turn to the question of functional completeness. If f is some n-ary truth function $f : \{\mathbf{T}, \mathbf{F}, \mathbf{N}, \mathbf{B}\}^n \to \{\mathbf{T}, \mathbf{F}, \mathbf{N}, \mathbf{B}\}$ and φ is some formula in which exactly the propositional constants $p_1, \ldots, p_n$ occur, we say that φ *expresses* f iff $\|\varphi\|^V = f(V(p_1), \ldots, V(p_n))$ for each valuation V. The following proposition holds (see the Appendix for its proof).

Theorem 4 *Every truth function is expressed by some formula.*

As a corollary we find that the set $\{\otimes, \lrcorner, \wedge, \neg\}$ is expressively adequate as well, since $\star$ is equivalent with $p_0 \otimes \neg \lrcorner p_0$, $\#$ is equivalent with $\lrcorner \star$ and

$$((\varphi @ \lrcorner \varphi) \leftrightarrow (\psi @ \lrcorner \psi)) \wedge ((\lrcorner \varphi @ \varphi) \leftrightarrow (\lrcorner \psi @ \psi))$$

is equivalent with $\varphi = \psi$.

So we can express all functions on the four truth combinations, but do we want this expressive power? Not all authors on partial logic seem to want full expressibility of all truth functions. Langholm 1988 e.g. considers only the classical connectives (except in his last chapter) and Blamey 1986 restricts himself to truth functions that are *monotonic*.

Definition 31 (Monotonic truth functions) An n-ary truth function f is called *monotonic* if it holds that

$$x_1 \sqsubseteq y_1, \ldots, x_n \sqsubseteq y_n \Rightarrow f(x_1, \ldots, x_n) \sqsubseteq f(y_1, \ldots, y_n)$$

for all $x_1, \ldots, x_n, y_1, \ldots, y_n \in \{\mathbf{T}, \mathbf{F}, \mathbf{N}, \mathbf{B}\}$.

There is a nice correspondence between monotonic truth functions and sentences that are built up using only $\star$, $\#$ and the classical $\wedge$, $\neg$ and $\top$.

Theorem 5 *A truth function is monotonic if and only if it is expressed by a sentence that is built up from propositional constants using only $\star$, $\#$, $\wedge$, $\neg$ and $\top$.*

The proof is Blamey's 1986, but I have adapted it to fit our four-valued logic; this adaptation can be found in the Appendix.

The monotonic truth functions are a natural enough class to consider. But for our purposes it will not do to restrict us to this set. There are truth functions that are not monotonic but that we want to be able to express nevertheless; the identity function, discussed above, is one of them, but there are other examples as well. Consider the following abbreviations.

Definition 32 (More abbreviations)

$\varphi \twoheadrightarrow \psi$ abbreviates $(\varphi \wedge \psi) = \varphi$
$\varphi \sqsubseteq \psi$ abbreviates $(\varphi \otimes \psi) = \varphi$

Clearly these are object-language versions of the ordering relations $\subseteq$ and $\sqsubseteq$ in the lattices L4 and A4 discussed above. (We let $\sqsubseteq$, like $\dashv$, do double duty as an object-language and a meta-language symbol; no confusion is likely to occur.) Here are the truth tables.

$\twoheadrightarrow$	**T**	**F**	**N**	**B**		$\sqsubseteq$	**T**	**F**	**N**	**B**
T	T	F	F	F		**T**	T	F	F	T
F	T	T	T	T		**F**	F	T	F	T
N	T	F	T	F		**N**	T	T	T	T
B	T	F	F	T		**B**	F	F	F	T

Since the double-headed arrow corresponds to the relation $\subseteq$ on the truth combinations it also corresponds to entailment; we have:

$$\varphi \models \psi \text{ if and only if } \models \varphi \twoheadrightarrow \psi.$$

The symbols $\twoheadrightarrow$ and $\sqsubseteq$ are very useful but they are not monotonic. In the rest of this book we shall have some occasion to use them; they must therefore be definable and we cannot restrict ourselves to the monotonic connectives.

The truth table for $\twoheadrightarrow$ given above is just the one that Anderson and Belnap 1975 associate with the notion of 'tautological entailment'.[6] Moreover, since these authors give an Extended Strong Kleene interpretation to conjunction, disjunction and negation, our partial propositional logic is in fact an extension[7] of the logic $\mathbf{E}_{fde}$ of tautological entailment (see Anderson and Belnap 1975, pp. 161–162). One of our motives to partialize classical logic has been our discontent with the coarse-grainedness of the classical relation of entailment. Some arguments that are classically valid are nevertheless irrelevant. (Examples are: $\models \varphi \vee \neg\varphi$; $\varphi \wedge \neg\varphi \models$ and $\varphi \wedge \neg\varphi \models \psi \vee \neg\psi$.) Since this irrelevance of classical entailment leads to

---

[6]Anderson and Belnap do not wish to distinguish between the meta-language $\models$ and the object-language $\twoheadrightarrow$; we do.

[7]A real extension since $\star$ and $\#$ cannot be expressed in Anderson and Belnaps logic. We also allow occurrences of the double arrow to be arbitrarily deeply nested.

problems if we use classical logic as an instrument to describe the semantics of natural language, we have wanted to get rid of it. The source of the irrelevance we have diagnosed to be the classical connection between truth and falsity. Giving up this connection indeed leads to a form of Relevant Logic.

Partial Predicate Logic

Having discussed partial propositional logic to some extent, we shall define its obvious extension to partial predicate logic. Let us start with the syntax. Assuming some countably infinite set of individual variables and a set L (a language) consisting of relation symbols (each having a fixed number of argument places) and individual constants (we omit function symbols), we define *terms* to be either individual constants or individual variables. The set of formulae we define with the help of a slight extension of the standard clauses.

Definition 33 The set of (*partial predicate logical*) *formulae* is defined with the following clauses:

   i. If R is an n-ary relation symbol and t_1, ..., t_n are terms then $Rt_1 \ldots t_n$ is an (atomic) formula;
   ii. If t_1 and t_2 are terms then $(t_1 = t_2)$ is an (atomic) formula;
   iii. $\#$ and $\star$ are (atomic) formulae;
   iv. If φ and ψ are formulae then $\neg\varphi$, $(\varphi \wedge \psi)$ and $(\varphi = \psi)$ are formulae;
   v. If φ is a formula and x is an individual variable, then $\forall x\, \varphi$ is a formula.

Note that the identity symbol may occur in two different contexts; in one it is intended to denote identity between individuals, in the other it denotes identity between combinations of truth values.

Next comes the semantics. We define an *interpretation function* for a set D in the standard way as a function I with domain L such that $I(c) \in D$ if c is an individual constant and $I(R) \in D^n$ if R is an n-ary relation symbol. But we need *two* interpretation functions for each model now: a *model* for partial predicate logic is a triple $\langle D, I^+, I^- \rangle$ where I^+ and I^- are interpretation functions for D. We stipulate that $I^+(c) = I^-(c)$ if c is an individual constant, but for relational symbols R the *denotation* $I^+(R)$ and the *antidenotation* $I^-(R)$ may differ: the denotation of a relation symbol consists of those tuples for which it is *true* that they stand in the relation, the antidenotation consists of the tuples for which this is *false*. As before truth and falsity are not connected in the classical way, it may be neither true nor false or it may be both true and false that some tuple stands in a certain relation.

Assignments for a given model $\langle D, I^+, I^- \rangle$ are defined as usual: they are functions taking variables to elements of D. If a is an assignment then

$a[d/x]$ is the assignment such that $a[d/x](x) = d$ and $a[d/x](y) = a(y)$ if $y \neq x$. The *value* of a term t in a model $M = \langle D, I^+, I^- \rangle$ under an assignment a, $\|t\|^{M,a}$, is defined as $I^+(t)$ (or, equivalently, as $I^-(t)$) if t is a constant and as $a(t)$ if t is a variable. On the basis of these definitions we can give truth conditions for our formulae.

Definition 34 (Tarski truth definition for partial predicate logic) The *value* $\|\varphi\|^{M,a} \in \{\mathbf{T}, \mathbf{F}, \mathbf{N}, \mathbf{B}\}$ of a formula φ on a model $M = \langle D, I^+, I^- \rangle$ under an assignment a is defined in the following way (I suppress superscripts where possible):

   i. $\|Rt_1 \ldots t_n\| = \mathbf{T}$ if $\langle \|t_1\|, \ldots, \|t_n\| \rangle \in I^+(R) - I^-(R)$,
     $\|Rt_1 \ldots t_n\| = \mathbf{F}$ if $\langle \|t_1\|, \ldots, \|t_n\| \rangle \in I^-(R) - I^+(R)$,
     $\|Rt_1 \ldots t_n\| = \mathbf{N}$ if $\langle \|t_1\|, \ldots, \|t_n\| \rangle \in D^n - (I^+(R) \cup I^-(R))$,
     $\|Rt_1 \ldots t_n\| = \mathbf{B}$ if $\langle \|t_1\|, \ldots, \|t_n\| \rangle \in I^+(R) \cap I^-(R)$;
   ii. $\|t_1 = t_2\| = \mathbf{T}$ if $\|t_1\| = \|t_2\|$,
     $\|t_1 = t_2\| = \mathbf{F}$ if $\|t_1\| \neq \|t_2\|$;
   iii. $\|\#\| = \mathbf{B}$;
     $\|\star\| = \mathbf{N}$;
   iv. $\|\neg\varphi\| = -\|\varphi\|$;
     $\|\varphi \wedge \psi\| = \|\varphi\| \cap \|\psi\|$;
     $\|\varphi = \psi\| = \mathbf{T}$ if $\|\varphi\| = \|\psi\|$,
     $\|\varphi = \psi\| = \mathbf{F}$ if $\|\varphi\| \neq \|\psi\|$;
   v. $\|\forall x\, \varphi\|^{M,a} = \bigcap_{d \in D} \|\varphi\|^{M, a[d/x]}$.

This definition is cast in a form that agrees with the format of the truth definition for partial propositional logic given above and also with the format of the corresponding definition for partial type theory that will be given in the next chapter, but we could easily have chosen a more familiar form since, as the reader can easily verify, the following equivalences obtain. (We write $M \models \varphi[a]$ if $\|\varphi\|^{M,a}$ includes truth and $M \dashv \varphi[a]$ if $\|\varphi\|^{M,a}$ includes falsity.)

   i. $M \models Rt_1 \ldots t_n[a]$ iff $\langle \|t_1\|, \ldots, \|t_n\| \rangle \in I^+(R)$;
     $M \dashv Rt_1 \ldots t_n[a]$ iff $\langle \|t_1\|, \ldots, \|t_n\| \rangle \in I^-(R)$;
   ii. $M \models t_1 = t_2[a]$ iff $\|t_1\| = \|t_2\|$
     $M \dashv t_1 = t_2[a]$ iff $\|t_1\| \neq \|t_2\|$;
   iii. $M \models \#[a]$
     $M \dashv \#[a]$;
     $M \not\models \star[a]$
     $M \not\dashv \star[a]$;
   iv. $M \models \neg\varphi[a]$ iff $M \dashv \varphi[a]$;
     $M \dashv \neg\varphi[a]$ iff $M \models \varphi[a]$
     $M \models \varphi \wedge \psi[a]$ iff $M \models \varphi[a]$ and $M \models \psi[a]$
     $M \dashv \varphi \wedge \psi[a]$ iff $M \dashv \varphi[a]$ or $M \dashv \psi[a]$;

$M \models \varphi = \psi[a]$ iff $\|\varphi\| = \|\psi\|$
$M \dashv \varphi = \psi[a]$ iff $\|\varphi\| \neq \|\psi\|$;

v. $M \models \forall x\,\varphi[a]$ iff $M \models \varphi[a[d/x]]$ for all $d \in D$
$M \dashv \forall x\,\varphi[a]$ iff $M \dashv \varphi[a[d/x]]$ for some $d \in D$.

Note that the definition does not only give the Extended Strong Kleene truth conditions to $\neg$ and $\wedge$, but to $\forall$ now as well: A universally quantified formula is true iff all its instances are true, false iff at least one of its instances is false. Again this condition is in fact the classical one; of course in the classical case one of the condition's conjuncts is superfluous. It is clear that clauses iii. and iv. are the only ones possible if we want the logic to be a generalization of the partial propositional logic discussed above. The form of clause i. is a direct consequence of the denotation-antidenotation approach, and clause ii. (a clause that is in analogy with the last clause of iv.) is again the only reasonable one if we want identity to satisfy the identity axioms.

Let us define entailment with the help of the L4 ordering relation again.

Definition 35 (Entailment in partial predicate logic) Let Γ and Δ be sets of formulae. Γ *entails* Δ, $\Gamma \models \Delta$, if

$$\bigcap_{\varphi \in \Gamma} \|\varphi\|^{M,a} \subseteq \bigcup_{\psi \in \Delta} \|\psi\|^{M,a}$$

for all models M and assignments a for M.

What are this logic's properties? I shall not go too deeply into this, since after all we are not after partial predicate logic for its own sake in this book, but want to use it as an intermediate station on our way to a formulation of the full partial theory of types. However, I want to give an embedding of partial predicate logic into ordinary predicate logic. This embedding is (a variation upon an embedding) due to Gilmore 1974 (see also Feferman 1984, Langholm 1988) and it can be used to reduce many questions about the partial theory to questions about the total one. With its help we can get some important theorems for free. The following definition gives the syntactic part.

Definition 36 With each n-ary relation symbol R of our language L we associate two n-ary symbols R^+ and R^-. Let $L^\dagger$ be the language consisting of (a) all relation symbols R^+ and R^- associated with some $R \in L$, (b) all individual constants in L and (c) two new zero place relation symbols p^+ and p. If φ is a formula then we write $\pm\varphi$ for the result of simultaneously substituting each R^+ for its associated R^- and each R^- for its associated R^+ in φ (p^+ and p^- are meant to be included here). With each formula φ of partial predicate logic we associate a formula $\varphi^\dagger$ of ordinary predicate logic with the help of the following clauses.

i. $(Rt_1 \ldots t_n)^{\dagger} = R^+ t_1 \ldots t_n;$

ii. $(t_1 = t_2)^{\dagger} = t_1 = t_2;$

iii. $(\#)^{\dagger} = p^+;$

   $(\star)^{\dagger} = p^-;$

iv. $(\neg\varphi)^{\dagger} = \neg \pm \varphi^{\dagger};$

   $(\varphi \wedge \psi)^{\dagger} = \varphi^{\dagger} \wedge \psi^{\dagger};$

   $(\varphi = \psi)^{\dagger} = (\varphi^{\dagger} \leftrightarrow \psi^{\dagger}) \wedge \pm(\varphi^{\dagger} \leftrightarrow \psi^{\dagger});$

v. $(\forall x\, \varphi)^{\dagger} = \forall x\, \varphi^{\dagger}.$

The following lemma holds.

Embedding Lemma. *Let $M_4 = \langle D, I^+, I^- \rangle$ be a model for partial predicate logic and let $M_2 = \langle D, I_2 \rangle$ be a model for standard predicate logic such that:*

(i.) $I_2(c) = I^+(c)$ for each individual constant $c \in L$;

(ii.) $I_2(p^+) = 1$, $I_2(p^-) = 0$;

(iii.) $I_2(R^+) = I^+(R)$ and $I_2(R^-) = D_n - I^-(R)$ for all n-ary relation symbols R.

Then the following two equivalences hold for each assignment a :

$$M_4 \models \varphi[a] \text{ iff } M_2 \models \varphi^{\dagger}[a]$$
$$M_4 \dashv \varphi[a] \text{ iff } M_2 \models \neg \pm \varphi^{\dagger}[a].$$

The proof of this lemma is a straightforward induction on the complexity of φ which we leave to the reader. From the Embedding Lemma the next theorem follows.

Theorem 6 (Embedding Theorem) *Let Γ and Δ be sets of sentences of partial predicate logic. Define $\Gamma^{\dagger}$ to be the set $\{\varphi^{\dagger} \mid \varphi \in \Gamma\}$ and similarly define $\Delta^{\dagger}$ to be $\{\psi^{\dagger} \mid \psi \in \Delta\}$. Write $\models_2$ for the relation of entailment in predicate logic. Then:*

$$\Gamma \models \Delta \text{ iff } \Gamma^{\dagger}, (p^+ \wedge \neg p^-) \vee (p^- \wedge \neg p^+) \models_2 \Delta^{\dagger}.$$

The proofs of this theorem and of its corollaries—see below—are in the Appendix as usual.

   We can in fact reap a rich harvest of corollaries. Let us call M a *model* of a theory Σ if $M \models \sigma$ for every $\sigma \in \Sigma$. We have:

Corollary. (Compactness Theorem for partial predicate logic) *If every finite subset of some theory has a model then that theory has a model.*

Corollary. (Löwenheim-Skolem Theorem for partial predicate logic) *If a theory has an infinite model then it has a countably infinite model.*

Corollary. *There is a recursive axiomatization of partial predicate logic.*

I shall not actually give an axiomatization. But in the next chapter we shall consider an axiomatization of partial type theory that can be simplified in an obvious way in order to get an axiomatization of partial predicate logic.

A simple but useful corollary is the following:

Corollary. *Let Γ and Δ be sets of sentences of partial predicate logic that are built up from $\neg$, $\wedge$, $\top$, $\bot$, $=$ and $\forall$. Then $\Gamma \models \Delta, \star$ iff $\Gamma, \star \models \Delta$.*

This last corollary is of some practical value since it follows that in many cases it will be possible to see that some entailment holds after doing only half of the checking that is required in general. If some argument consists only of sentences built up from $\neg$, $\wedge$, $\top$, $\bot$, $=$ and $\forall$, then it suffices to prove either that truth is preserved from premises to conclusions or that falsity is preserved in the other direction. We need not prove both in these cases because either proposition implies the other.

We opened this chapter questioning one of the central principles of classical logic, the principle that a sentence is true if and only if it is not false. What happens if we drop this principle? We can now, closing the chapter, give a general answer to this question. The answer is: surprisingly little. Giving up the classical connection between truth and falsity leads to a version of predicate logic that is in many respects still very close to the standard version. There is a simple function embedding the former logic into the latter and we can use this embedding in many cases to reduce questions about four-valued predicate logic to questions about standard logic.

6

Going Partial II: Type Theory

We shall now apply the findings of the previous Chapter to the theory of types. This can be done in two ways. We can apply them to the relational formulation of type theory that we have met with in Chapter 2 above and we can apply them to the more standard functional formulation. We shall do both but we shall start with an application to the latter theory.

Defining a four-valued variant of functional type logic is a rather straightforward exercise. The idea is that we let the models of this logic be defined just as TY_2 models are, except that this time we let the type t domain consist of the set of the four truth combinations instead of the set of truth values. We can then use the ideas discussed in the previous chapter to define how terms are evaluated on these models. We shall call the logic TY_2^4 (four-valued two-sorted functional type theory). Here is a definition of the four-valued frames.

Definition 37 (TY_2^4 frames) A (*standard*) TY_2^4 *frame* is a set of sets $\{D_\alpha \mid \alpha$ is a functional type$\}$ such that $D_e \neq \emptyset$, $D_s \neq \emptyset$, $D_t = \{\mathbf{T}, \mathbf{F}, \mathbf{N}, \mathbf{B}\}$ and $D_{\alpha\beta}$ is the set of (total) functions from D_α to D_β.

TY_2^4 *standard models* and *assignments* are defined from these in the obvious way. TY_2^4 terms are just ordinary TY_2 terms, except that $\#$ and $\star$ are now stipulated to be TY_2^4 formulae (type t terms). TY_2^4 terms can be evaluated on TY_2^4 models with the help of the Strong Kleene operations.

Definition 38 (Tarski truth definition for TY_2^4) The *value* $|A|^{M,a}$ of a term A on a TY_2^4 standard model $M = \langle \{D_\alpha\}_\alpha, I \rangle$ under an assignment a is defined as follows:

   i. $|c| = I(c)$ if c is a constant;
     $|x| = a(x)$ if x is a variable;

   ii. $|\neg\varphi| = -|\varphi|$;
     $|\varphi \wedge \psi| = |\varphi| \cap |\varphi|$;
     $|\#| = \mathbf{B}$;
     $|\star| = \mathbf{N}$;

iii. $|\forall x_\alpha \, \varphi|^{M,a} = \bigcap_{d \in D_\alpha} |\varphi|^{M,a[d/x]}$;

iv. $|A_{\alpha\beta}B_\alpha| = |A|(|B|)$;

v. $|\lambda x_\alpha \, A_\beta|^{M,a} =$ the $F \in D_{\alpha\beta}$ such that for all $d \in D_\beta$: $F(d) = |A|^{M,a[d/x]}$;

vi. $|A = B| = \mathbf{T}$ if $|A| = |B|$
$= \mathbf{F}$ if $|A| \neq |B|$.

The operations $-$, $\cap$ and $\bigcap$ are again operations in the logical algebra LK4 here, just as the operation $\bigcup$ in the following definition is (while $\subseteq$ is the ordering relation on L4). The definition stipulates that the relation of entailment is the double-barrelled one again:

Definition 39 (Entailment in TY_2^4) Let Γ and Δ be sets of TY_2^4 formulae. The relation $\Gamma \models_s \Delta$ holds in TY_2^4 if

$$\bigcap_{\varphi \in \Gamma} |\varphi|^{M,a} \subseteq \bigcup_{\psi \in \Delta} |\psi|^{M,a}$$

for all TY_2^4 standard models M and assignments a to M.

This defines the logic. Question: Is this the kind of logic that we are after? Is this really a *partial* theory of types? The answer is yes if we apply the criterion given in the first pages of Chapter 5, for this is a logic in which the classical connection between truth and falsity has been given up and in which truth combinations replace truth values. But there is doubt: All functions in the models of this logic are total functions. Worse, although functions of certain types could be interpreted as partial objects—type *et* functions for example can be interpreted as partial sets (see below)—other functions in other types cannot possibly be viewed in such a way—total functions of type *ee*, for example, remain total objects, no matter in what way we look at them.

Setting this problem aside for a moment (we shall return to it below), we turn to the task of partializing the relational variant of type theory. This time, since *t* is no longer a basic type, we cannot define the models of the theory by simply replacing their domain of truth values with the set of truth combinations and leaving everything else as it was before. We can however partialize the objects that all non-basic domains consist of— relations. Here is the definition of a partial relation.

Definition 40 (Partial relations) Let $D_1, \ldots, D_n$ be sets. An n-ary *partial relation* R on $D_1, \ldots, D_n$ is a tuple $\langle R^+, R^- \rangle$ of relations R^+, $R^- \subseteq D_1 \times \ldots \times D_n$. The relation R^+ is called R's *denotation*; R^- is called R's *antidenotation*, the relation $(D_1 \times \ldots \times D_n) - (R^+ \cup R^-)$ (written $(R^+ \cup R^-)^c$) its *gap*; and $R^+ \cap R^-$ its *glut*. A partial relation is *coherent* if its glut is empty, *total* if its gap is empty, *incoherent* if it is not coherent and *classical* if it is both coherent and total. A unary partial relation is called a *partial set*.

If D is some set then the *partial power set* of D, $PPow(D)$, is $Pow(D) \times Pow(D)$, the set $\{\langle R^+, R^- \rangle \mid R^+, R^- \subseteq D\}$ of all partial sets over D.

The idea here, as it was in the case of partial predicate logic, is that it is true of a tuple of objects that they stand in a partial relation R if they are in R's denotation and that it is false that they stand in R if they are in its antidenotation. This of course leaves open the possibility that it is neither true nor false that a given tuple stand in R or that it is both true and false that they do.

The natural operations on the set of truth combinations $\{\mathbf{T}, \mathbf{F}, \mathbf{N}, \mathbf{B}\}$ that we have defined in the previous chapter can be extended to the class of partial relations. The Extended Strong Kleene valuation scheme for example leads to a generalization of the usual Boolean operations on ordinary relations.

Definition 41 Let $R_1 = \langle R_1^+, R_1^- \rangle$ and $R_2 = \langle R_2^+, R_2^- \rangle$ be partial relations. Define:

$$-R_1 \quad := \quad \langle R_1^-, R_1^+ \rangle \text{ (partial complementation)}$$
$$R_1 \cap R_2 \quad := \quad \langle R_1^+ \cap R_2^+, R_1^- \cup R_2^- \rangle \text{ (partial intersection)}$$
$$R_1 \cup R_2 \quad := \quad \langle R_1^+ \cup R_2^+, R_1^- \cap R_2^- \rangle \text{ (partial union)}$$
$$R_1 \subseteq R_2 \quad \text{iff} \quad R_1^+ \subseteq R_2^+ \text{ and } R_2^- \subseteq R_1^- \text{ (partial inclusion)}$$

Let A be some set of partial relations. Define:

$$\bigcap A \quad := \quad \langle \bigcap \{R^+ \mid R \in A\}, \bigcup \{R^- \mid R \in A\} \rangle$$
$$\bigcup A \quad := \quad \langle \bigcup \{R^+ \mid R \in A\}, \bigcap \{R^- \mid R \in A\} \rangle.$$

Consider that it is true of a tuple of objects that they stand in the partial relation $-R$ iff it is false that they stand in R, false that they stand in $-R$ iff it is true that they stand in R. It is true of a tuple of objects that they stand in $R_1 \cap R_2$ iff it is both true that they stand in R_1 and that they stand in R_2; false that they stand in $R_1 \cap R_2$ iff it is false that they stand in R_1 or false that they stand in R_2, etcetera. Note that a set of partial relations on domains $D_1, \ldots, D_n$ that is closed under the operations $\cap$, $\cup$ and $-$ and that contains $\langle \emptyset, D_1 \times \ldots \times D_n \rangle$ and $\langle D_1 \times \ldots \times D_n, \emptyset \rangle$ forms a Kleene algebra. We shall call any Kleene algebra that has this particular form a *natural Kleene algebra on a set of partial relations*. The converse of the observation that we have just made holds as well: By a trivial adaptation of the proof of the Stone Representation Theorem for Boolean algebras we see that any Kleene algebra can be represented by a natural Kleene algebra on a set of partial relations.

Theorem 7 (Representation Theorem for Kleene algebras) *Every Kleene algebra is isomorphic to a natural Kleene algebra on a set of partial sets.*

The proof can again be found in the Appendix.

These were the LK4 operations generalized to the class of partial relations, but in a similar way the operations in the approximation algebra AK4 can be generalized to form operations on this class.

Definition 42 Let $R_1 = \langle R_1^+, R_1^- \rangle$ and $R_2 = \langle R_2^+, R_2^- \rangle$ be partial relations. Define:

$$
\begin{aligned}
\lrcorner R_1 &:= \langle (R_1^-)^c, (R_1^+)^c \rangle \\
R_1 \sqcap R_2 &:= \langle R_1^+ \cap R_2^+, R_1^- \cap R_2^- \rangle \\
R_1 \sqcup R_2 &:= \langle R_1^+ \cup R_2^+, R_1^- \cup R_2^- \rangle \\
R_1 \sqsubseteq R_2 &\quad\text{iff}\quad R_1^+ \subseteq R_2^+ \text{ and } R_1^- \subseteq R_2^- \quad (R_1 \text{ approximates } R_2)
\end{aligned}
$$

This time we see that a set of partial relations on domains $D_1, \ldots, D_n$ that is closed under the operations $\sqcap$, $\sqcup$ and $\lrcorner$ and that contains the partial relations $\langle \emptyset, \emptyset \rangle$ and $\langle D_1 \times \ldots \times D_n, D_1 \times \ldots \times D_n \rangle$ forms a Kleene algebra. Now that we have partial relations and some structure on them let us use them to build up our frames again.

Definition 43 (Frames) A *frame* is a set $\{D_\alpha \mid \alpha \text{ is a type}\}$ such that $D_e \neq \emptyset$, $D_s \neq \emptyset$ and

$$
D_{\langle \alpha_1 \ldots \alpha_n \rangle} \subseteq PPow(D_{\alpha_1} \times \ldots \times D_{\alpha_n}).
$$

A frame is *standard* if $D_{\langle \alpha_1 \ldots \alpha_n \rangle} = PPow(D_{\alpha_1} \times \ldots \times D_{\alpha_n})$ for all $\alpha_1, \ldots, \alpha_n$.

In a (standard) frame each domain $D_{\langle \alpha_1 \ldots \alpha_n \rangle}$ now consists of (all the) partial relations on domains $D_{\alpha_1}, \ldots, D_{\alpha_n}$. Note that since the relational domains of a frame are defined as arbitrary subsets of the relevant partial power set, it need not be the case that they are closed under the operations $\cap$, $\cup$, $-$, $\sqcap$, $\sqcup$ and $\lrcorner$. However, we shall shortly restrict our attention to a class of frames in which each relational domain is thus closed.

Checking the set $PPow(\{\emptyset\})$ we see the truth-combinations **T**, **F**, **N** and **B** reappear. The set's four elements are $\langle 1, 0 \rangle$, $\langle 0, 1 \rangle$, $\langle 0, 0 \rangle$ and $\langle 1, 1 \rangle$, which we shall interpret as 'true and not false', 'false and not true', 'true nor false' and 'both true and false' respectively. (If a value's first element is 1, it includes truth; if its second element is 1, it includes falsity.) The operations $\cap$, $\cup$ and $-$ give the logical algebra LK4 on the set (modulo isomorfism) and $\sqcap$, $\sqcup$ and $\lrcorner$ give the approximation algebra AK4. Although, as we have seen above, in functional type theory it will not do to define the basic domain D_t as $\{\mathbf{T}, \mathbf{F}, \mathbf{N}, \mathbf{B}\}$ in order to get a partialization of objects in all complex domains, in the relational theory a partialization of the relations in all non-basic domains leads to the desired shape of $D_{\langle\rangle}$.

In Chapter 2 we have seen that there is a converse to Schönfinkel's way of identifying relations with unary functions. Instead of trading relations for functions, we have decided to keep the relations and do away with the functions there. But the possibility of doing this rested completely on the existence of the slice functions we defined. And so, since we now want to base the logic on partial instead of classical relations, the definition of slice functions must be extended.

Definition 44 (Slice Functions) Let R be an n-ary partial relation and let $0 < k \leq n$. The *k-th slice function* F_R^k of R is defined by $F_R^k(d) = \langle F_{R+}^k(d), F_{R-}^k(d) \rangle$.

A picture may again help to see what is going on.

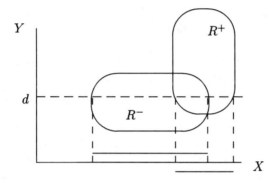

A binary partial relation on the reals can this time be identified with a pair of sets (a partial set) in the Euclidean plane. This pair of sets can be viewed as a (total) function that sends any point on the Y-axis to a pair of sets of points on the X-axis. So it is a function from points on the Y-axis to partial sets of points on the X-axis.

We are ready to give a Tarski truth definition evaluating the syntax of ordinary type theory on partial frames. To the language of TT_2 we again add the two logical constants, # and $\star$, both of formula type $\langle \rangle$. A *very general model* is a tuple $\langle F, I \rangle$ where $F = \{D_\alpha\}_\alpha$ is a partial frame and I is an interpretation function for F. A very general model is called *standard* if its frame is standard.[1]

---

[1]The name *standard* model is conventional, it should not be taken to imply any preference on our part. On the contrary, it is well known that a restriction to standard models introduces all kinds of inconstructivities into the theory. One gains expressive power and as a consequence one loses the recursive axiomatizability of entailment and the Löwenheim-Skolem theorem. In view of this we prefer not to make such a restriction at all in the present context. (See Van Benthem and Doets 1983 for a discussion of the

Definition 45 (Tarski truth definition) The *value* $\|A\|^{M,a}$ of a term A on a very general model M under an assignment a is defined in the following way:

   i. $\|c\| = I(c)$ if c is a constant;
      $\|x\| = a(x)$ if x is a variable;

  ii. $\|\neg\varphi\| = -\|\varphi\|$;
      $\|\varphi \wedge \psi\| = \|\varphi\| \cap \|\psi\|$;
      $\|\#\| = \langle 1,1 \rangle$;
      $\|\star\| = \langle 0,0 \rangle$;

 iii. $\|\forall x_\alpha\, \varphi\|^{M,a} = \bigcap_{d \in D_\alpha} \|\varphi\|^{M,a[d/x]}$;

 iv. $\|AB\| = F^1_{\|A\|}(\|B\|)$;

  v. $\|\lambda x_\beta\, A\|^{M,a} = $ the R such that $F^1_R(d) = \|A\|^{M,a[d/x]}$ for all $d \in D_\beta$;

 vi. $\|A = B\| = \langle 1,0 \rangle$ if $\|A\| = \|B\|$
            $= \langle 0,1 \rangle$ if $\|A\| \neq \|B\|$.

Note that in general there is no guarantee that the value of a term will be an element of the appropriate domain. Still the notion is well-defined. We are however mainly interested in very general models M such that $\|A_\alpha\|^{M,a} \in D_\alpha$ for all terms A and all assignments a; we shall call these *general models* or just *models*.

    Relational domains of general models are closed under the operations $\cap$, $\cup$, $-$, $\sqcap$, $\sqcup$ and $\dashv$. For example if the variables R and R' denote partial relations of some n-ary type, then the term $\lambda x_1 \ldots x_n\, (Rx_1 \ldots x_n \vee R'x_1 \ldots x_n)$ will denote their partial disjunction. For the other cases use the connectives $\wedge$, $\neg$, $\otimes$, $\oplus$ and $\dashv$.

    We define the notion of entailment in the double-barrelled way again, using the partial analogues in LK4 of the Boolean operations instead of these operations themselves.

Definition 46 Let Γ and Δ be sets of terms of some type $\alpha = \langle \alpha_1 \ldots \alpha_n \rangle$. Γ (*s-*) *entails* Δ, $\Gamma \models \Delta$ ($\Gamma \models_s \Delta$), if

$$\bigcap_{A \in \Gamma} \|A\|^{M,a} \subseteq \bigcup_{B \in \Delta} \|B\|^{M,a}$$

for all (standard) models M and assignments a to M.

The logical system thus defined we call TT^4_2 .

    How wild is the relation of logical consequence $\models$? Not very. We shall characterize it (or rather its restriction to formulae) with the help of a rather familiar-looking calculus of sequents. (In these rules the notation $[A/x]B$ presupposes that A is substitutable for x in B.)

---

point.) Allowing domains to be only a part of the full power set of the relevant Cartesian product seems to fit in nicely with the general spirit of partial semantics.

R

$$\varphi \Rightarrow \varphi$$

Cut

$$\frac{\Gamma, \varphi \Rightarrow \Delta \quad \Gamma \Rightarrow \varphi, \Delta}{\Gamma \Rightarrow \Delta}$$

Thinning

$$\frac{\Gamma \Rightarrow \Delta}{\Gamma, \varphi \Rightarrow \Delta} \qquad \frac{\Gamma \Rightarrow \Delta}{\Gamma \Rightarrow \Delta, \varphi}$$

Negation Rules

$$\frac{\{\neg\gamma \mid \gamma \in \Gamma\} \Rightarrow \Delta}{\{\neg\delta \mid \delta \in \Delta\} \Rightarrow \Gamma} \qquad \frac{\Gamma \Rightarrow \{\neg\delta \mid \delta \in \Delta\}}{\Delta \Rightarrow \{\neg\gamma \mid \gamma \in \Gamma\}}$$

Truth value Rules

$$\Rightarrow \varphi = \top, \varphi = \bot, \varphi = \star, \varphi = \# \qquad \Rightarrow \star = \neg\star$$
$$\text{(Excluded Fifth)} \qquad\qquad\qquad\qquad \Rightarrow \# = \neg\#$$
$$\Rightarrow \#, \star$$

Conjunction Rules

$$\mathrm{E}\wedge \quad \frac{\Gamma, \varphi, \psi \Rightarrow \Delta}{\Gamma, \varphi \wedge \psi \Rightarrow \Delta} \qquad \mathrm{I}\wedge \quad \varphi, \psi \Rightarrow \varphi \wedge \psi$$

Quantifier Rules

$$\mathrm{I}\forall \quad \frac{\Gamma \Rightarrow [c/x]\varphi, \Delta}{\Gamma \Rightarrow \forall x\, \varphi, \Delta} \qquad \mathrm{E}\forall \quad \forall x\, \varphi \Rightarrow [A/x]\varphi$$

provided c does not occur in Γ or Δ.

Identity Rules

$$\Rightarrow A = A$$
$$A = B, [A/x]\varphi \Rightarrow [B/x]\varphi \qquad \text{(Leibniz's Law)}$$

Beta-conversion

$$\Rightarrow \lambda x\, (A)B = [B/x]A$$

Extensionality

$$\forall x\, (Ax = Bx) \Rightarrow A = B, \text{ provided } x \text{ is not free in } A \text{ or } B.$$

By inspection it is seen that the rules of this calculus preserve entailment. That is, if

$$\Gamma_1 \Rightarrow \Delta_1, \ldots, \Gamma_n \Rightarrow \Delta_n / \Gamma_{n+1} \Rightarrow \Delta_{n+1}$$

is a rule (n possibly being equal to 0 and never being greater than 2) and if

$$\Gamma_1 \models \Delta_1, \ldots, \Gamma_n \models \Delta_n$$

hold, then $\Gamma_{n+1} \models \Delta_{n+1}$ holds as well. To see this one must in some cases use the following theorem, which can be proved by a straightforward induction on term complexity:

Theorem 8 (Substitution Theorem) *If A is substitutable for x in B then* $\|[A/x]B\|^{M,a} = \|B\|^{M,a[d/x]}$, *where* $d = \|A\|^{M,a}$.

We say that a sequent is *provable* if it belongs to the smallest set of sequents that is closed under the rules above. Note that if $\Gamma \Rightarrow \Delta$ is provable, then Γ and Δ are both finite. Write $\Pi \vdash \Sigma$ if there are Π_0 and Σ_0 such that $\Pi_0 \subseteq \Pi$, $\Sigma_0 \subseteq \Sigma$ and $\Pi_0 \Rightarrow \Sigma_0$ is provable. Clearly $\Pi \models \Sigma$ (and hence $\Pi \models_s \Sigma$), if $\Pi \vdash \Sigma$.

In the case of $\models$ the converse also holds.

Theorem 9 (Generalized Completeness Theorem) *Let Π and Σ be sets of formulae then:*

$$\Pi \vdash \Sigma \Leftrightarrow \Pi \models \Sigma.$$

The proof is in the Appendix. Varying slightly on it, we get proofs of generalized completeness theorems for the two-valued and the three-valued variants of the present logic as well. In particular, let $\vdash_2$ be defined as the relation $\vdash$ above (restricted to formulae that do not contain $\star$ or $\#$), except that this time we let the Truth Value Rules consist of the single sequent

$$\Rightarrow \varphi = \mathsf{T}, \varphi = \perp.$$

Then we have:

Corollary (Generalized Completeness Theorem for TT_2) *Let Π and Σ be sets of TT_2 formulae and let $\models_2$ be the relation of generalized entailment in TT_2 (defined in a way analogous to the definition of $\models$ in TT_2^4), then:*

$$\Pi \vdash_2 \Sigma \Leftrightarrow \Pi \models_2 \Sigma.$$

For the three-valued variant of the logic, consider terms that do not contain $\#$ (but may contain $\star$) and revise the definition of *frame* so that each relational domain may consist only of coherent relations:

Definition 47 (Three-Valued Frames) A *three-valued frame* is a set

$$\{D_\alpha \mid \alpha \text{ is a type}\}$$

such that $D_e \neq \emptyset$, $D_s \neq \emptyset$ and for each $\alpha_1, \ldots, \alpha_n$:

$$D_{\langle \alpha_1 \ldots \alpha_n \rangle} \subseteq \{\langle R^+, R^- \rangle \mid R^+, R^- \subseteq D_{\alpha_1} \times \ldots \times D_{\alpha_n} \text{ and } R^+ \cap R^- = \emptyset\}.$$

Write $\models_3$ for the (generalized) notion of logical consequence that results from this (temporary) revision. Call the resulting logic TT_2^3. On terms not containing $\#$ the relation $\models_3$ is weaker than $\models$. We have for instance that $\varphi \wedge \neg\varphi \models_3 \psi \vee \neg\psi$ but not $\varphi \wedge \neg\varphi \models \psi \vee \neg\psi$. We can characterize the relation $\models_3$ syntactically with the help of the derivability notion $\vdash_3$, where $\vdash_3$ is defined as $\vdash$ is, except that this time the following sequents form the Truth Value Rules.

$$\Rightarrow \quad \varphi = \mathsf{T}, \varphi = \perp, \varphi = \star$$
$$\Rightarrow \quad \star = \neg\star$$

We have:

Corollary (Generalized Completeness Theorem for TT_2^3) *Let Π and Σ be sets of TT_2^3 formulae then:*

$$\Pi \vdash_3 \Sigma \;\Leftrightarrow\; \Pi \models_3 \Sigma.$$

I leave the proofs of these corollaries to the reader.

Having characterized the consequence relation of (relational) partial type theory and its coherent and classical variants thus, we return to the four-valued *functional* theory of types TY_2^4 and to the question of its correct interpretation. Is it a partial type logic, despite of the fact that all domains consist of total objects? The following theorem clarifies the situation. The relation between TT_2^4 and TY_2^4 mirrors the relation between the total theories TT_2 and TY_2 exactly:

Theorem 10 *Let Π and Σ be sets of TT_2^4 sentences, then:*

$$\Pi \models_s \Sigma \; in \; TT_2^4 \;\Leftrightarrow\; \Pi \models_s \Sigma \; in \; TY_2^4.$$

The proof of this theorem is virtually the same as the proof of Theorem 1, so there is no need to spell it out. From this theorem we see that those total functions in TY_2^4 frames that have types in which no e or s immediately precedes a right parenthesis correspond to partial relations. Many other functions in these frames however (functions of type ee for example), do not correspond to partial relations in this way.

7

Situations, Persistence and Weak Consequence

Situations and the part-of relation

Why is it that in possible world semantics we can give the grand name of *possible worlds* to indices—the latter being after all nothing but primitive objects without internal structure? The answer is that indices correspond to *models* and that models far more deserve to be called worlds than indices at first blush seem to do.

Let us rehearse in some detail, working in the total theory given in Chapters 2 and 4 for the moment, what this correspondence between indices and models amounts to. Define the *extension* of a term A of type $\langle \alpha_1 \ldots \alpha_n s \rangle$ in index i in a model $M = \langle \{D_\alpha\}_\alpha, I \rangle$ under an assignment a as the relation $F_R^{n+1}(i)$ of type $\langle \alpha_1 \ldots \alpha_n \rangle$ such that $R = \|A\|^{M,a}$. The extension of the term $love_{\langle ees \rangle}$ in a given index i, for example, is $F_{\|love\|}^3(i)$, intuitively the set of pairs $\langle x, y \rangle$ such that x loves y in that index. With each index $i \in D_s$ we may now associate an interpretation function I_i thus:

$I_i(c) = I(c)$, if c is a constant of type e or type s;

$I_i(c) = $ the extension of the m-th constant of type $\langle \alpha_1 \ldots \alpha_n s \rangle$ in index i, if c is the m-th constant of type $\langle \alpha_1 \ldots \alpha_n \rangle$.

The idea is that we want the functions I_i to link the constants that were used in the translation of our PTQ fragment (the constants $love_{\langle ees \rangle}$, $man_{\langle es \rangle}$, $try_{\langle \langle es \rangle es \rangle}$ etc.), all having types of the form $\langle \alpha_1 \ldots \alpha_n s \rangle$, to their extensions in index i. This cannot be done in a direct way for the obvious reason that a constant and its extension will have different types. Therefore we let our constants correspond to constants of the right type (say: $\text{LOVE}_{\langle ee \rangle}$, $\text{MAN}_{\langle e \rangle}$, $\text{TRY}_{\langle \langle es \rangle e \rangle}$, ...) in a one-to-one fashion and send the latter to the extensions of the former.

Since the above construction gives us an interpretation function I_i for each index i, we now have a model corresponding to each index: define M_i

to be the model $\langle\{D_\alpha\}_\alpha, I_i\rangle$. An ordinary model M for two-sorted type theory can thus be viewed as what is called the *indexed union*[1] of a set of such models, one for each index. It is this simple trick that enables us to quantify over models (via quantification over indices) in possible world semantics.

What happens when we partialize the logic and repeat the construction given above using the definitions given in Chapter 6 instead of those in Chapter 2? Then the model M will be a partial model and the models M_i that constitute M as their indexed union will be partial too. They will still be possible worlds, but not necessarily fully specified or coherent ones, extensions at any index need no longer be classical. Hence they will be partial possible worlds, or, as I shall call them, (possible) situations. Since each M_i is completely given by its index i, we can identify indices with possible situations as well.

Once we have made this identification, our category-to-type assignment automatically associates categories of expressions in natural language with certain kinds of partial objects that are constructed out of situations and possible individuals. For example, sentences are now associated with partial sets of situations[2] (type $\langle s\rangle$ objects, propositions); common nouns and intransitive verb phrases are linked to functions from situations to partial sets of individuals (properties, type $\langle es\rangle$ objects); noun phrases to quantifiers, functions from situations to partial sets of properties (type $\langle\langle es\rangle s\rangle$ objects) and so on. The translation function $^\circ$ defined in Chapter 4 now assigns a partial relation of some kind to each analysis tree in each partial model.

Situations come with a natural structure. We say that a partial model $M_i = \langle\{D_\alpha\}_\alpha, I_i\rangle$ is *part of* a partial model $M_j = \langle\{D_\alpha\}_\alpha, I_j\rangle$ (or that M_j *extends* M_i) if $I_i(c) = I_j(c)$ for all constants c of basic types e or s and $I_i(c) \sqsubseteq I_j(c)$ for all constants c of relational type. Intuitively, M_j extends M_i if M_j is at least as defined as M_i is, or, to use a more dynamic picture, if M_i can grow into M_j.

The part-of relation is a relation between *models*, but since we view our models as the indexed unions of certain sets of models and have thus identified the indices *in* a model with certain models, the type s domain of any model inherits the structure and is ordered by a part-of relation too. In order to be able to express things about this relation in the object language, we introduce a non-logical constant $\leq$ of type $\langle ss\rangle$ and we shall make it behave like the part-of relation. Remember that in Chapter 5 above we have defined an object-language version $\sqsubseteq$ of the ordering relation in the

---

[1] See Barwise 1974 for this notion.

[2] This is as it should be if we want to embed (a part of) Situation Semantics into our theory: see Perry 1986.

Constants	Type
run, walk, talk	$\langle es \rangle$
find, lose, eat, love, date	$\langle ees \rangle$
conceive	$\langle \langle \langle es \rangle s \rangle es \rangle$
rapidly, slowly, voluntarily, allegedly	$\langle \langle es \rangle es \rangle$
man, woman, park, fish, pen, unicorn	$\langle es \rangle$
in	$\langle e \langle es \rangle es \rangle$
about	$\langle \langle \langle es \rangle s \rangle \langle es \rangle es \rangle$
believe	$\langle \langle s \rangle es \rangle$
assert, try, wish	$\langle \langle es \rangle es \rangle$
E	$\langle es \rangle$
B, K, A, see	$\langle ess \rangle$
Aristotle, John, Bill, Mary	$\langle es \rangle$
ρ	$\langle ss \rangle$.

TABLE 5

approximation lattice A4. The formula $\varphi \sqsubseteq \psi$, a formula that is always either true and not false or false and not true, may be read as 'φ approximates ψ'. More generally we can use $\forall x_1 \ldots x_n \, (cx_1 \ldots x_n i \sqsubseteq cx_1 \ldots x_n j)$ to express that the extension of constant c at index i approximates its extension at index j. Now define Ψ as the conjunction of all formulae of this form $\forall x_1 \ldots x_n \, (cx_1 \ldots x_n i \sqsubseteq cx_1 \ldots x_n j)$, where c is an element of the finite set of constants (the language) L defined in Table 5.

So Ψ is defined as the finite conjunction of $\forall xy \, (find \, xyi \sqsubseteq find \, xyj)$, $\forall x \, (man \, xi \sqsubseteq man \, xj)$, $\forall P \forall x \, (try \, Pxi \sqsubseteq try \, Pxj)$ etc. and since L consists of all constants of relational type that were used in translating the basic expressions of the PTQ fragment (plus some extra ones that we shall need in the next Chapters), the formula Ψ expresses that the extension of every relevant constant at index i approximates the extension of that constant at j. In other words, Ψ expresses that i is a part of j. The following axiom (or definition) makes $\leq$ behave the way we want it to.

AX9 $\forall ij \, (i \leq j = \Psi)$.

Clearly, in any model satisfying AX9 the part-of relation, the value of $\leq$, is a reflexive and transitive classical relation, it inherits these traits from the relation $\sqsubseteq$ in the approximation lattice A4 on the truth combinations, in terms of which it is defined.

Persistence

We can view the relation $\leq$ among indices as one of *growth of information*; and if we do a natural question comes to mind, a question related to the topic of monotonicity discussed in Chapter 5. If information grows, will true expressions remain true, will false expressions remain false, or will there be sentences whose truth value is instable? In order to formulate this question in a more precise way define a term A of type $\langle \alpha_1 \ldots \alpha_n s \rangle$ to be $\leq$-*persistent* if it holds that

$$\text{AX9} \models \forall ij\,(i \leq j \rightarrow \forall x_1 \ldots x_n(Ax_1 \ldots x_ni \sqsubseteq Ax_1 \ldots x_nj)).$$

In other words, A is $\leq$-persistent if its extension at any index i approximates its extension at j, if i is part of j. By AX9, all constants in the fragment $\leq$-persist, but does the property hold for translations of sentences as well? The answer is yes.

Theorem 11 ($\leq$-Persistency Theorem) *If ϑ is an analysis tree of category S, then its translation $\vartheta°$ (defined in Chapter 4) $\leq$-persists:*

$$\text{AX9} \models \forall ij\,(i \leq j \rightarrow (\vartheta°i \sqsubseteq \vartheta°j)).$$

So if a sentence is true (or false) at a certain situation it will remain so at all situations that extend it. Truth and falsity of sentences are retained under increase of definedness.

This, it might be argued, may not be the result we want. There are sentences in our fragment, sentences formed with the help of the determiners every, a and the, that are sometimes thought not to persist (see e.g. Perry 1986). While sentence (20), once it is false in some situation, will always remain false if that situation is enlarged, it could, so it is argued, be true at an index that is included in a situation at which it is no longer true. Conversely, sentence (21) could be false in some situation, but no longer so in an extension of it, while, once true, it will always remain true. Sentence (22) behaves even worse, it may lose its truth if the situation at which it is evaluated is extended, but in similar cases it may lose falsity too.

(20) Every man loves Mary

(21) Some woman talks

(22) The woman does not talk

But what is the nature of the growth we are talking about now? For the sake of clarity I think it is useful to distinguish between two ways in which one situation can be said to be 'larger' than a second one. The first of these ways we have discussed above, a situation is part of another if it is less defined than it. The second way is different from the first; it has to do with *growth of domain* rather than with growth of information.

Consider the situation associated with someone's field of vision. True, this visual scene may be less defined than the world itself is. To use one of Barwise's 1981 examples, even if Whitehead winks, Russell can see Whitehead without seeing him wink. But there is another important difference between the situation that Russell sees and the world in which he sees it, a difference that is so obvious that we might well overlook it. Characteristically we see only a very small portion of the world surrounding us. Hence our visual scene is not only *less defined* than the actual world is, it is also smaller in the sense that it contains *less objects*. Its domain is contained in (and is usually much smaller than) the set of all existing things. In cases like these we shall say that the smaller situation is *included* in the larger one.

There is a standard method that enables us to talk about indices that have varying domains; we can introduce an *existence predicate E*, technically a non-logical constant of type $\langle es \rangle$ that is to have the domain of each index as its extension at that index. The formula Exi we interpret as 'x exists in situation i' (in Situation Semantical terminology: 'x is *in* situation i'). The predicate distinguishes between those objects that are actual in a given situation and those that are merely possible. We want existence to be a classical predicate in the sense that it is always either true and not false or false and not true that some object exists. This is enforced with the help of the following stipulation.

AX10 $\forall xi\,(Exi = \top \vee Exi = \bot)$

Note that above we have listed E as a member of the language L. As a consequence AX9 assures the $\leq$-persistence of E. Together with our new axiom this means that if some situation is part of another both have the same domain: $\forall ij\,(i \leq j \rightarrow \forall x\,(Exi = Exj))$ is now derivable.

Clearly, if one situation is included in another, the domain of the latter must contain that of the former. But inclusion of domains is no sufficient condition for the relation of inclusion between situations to obtain. Other things must remain equal. For example, if John exists in situation i and if j includes i then it should be the case that 'John walks' is true (false) in i if and only if it is true (false) in j.

Let us define the notion of inclusion between situations. Consider for each constant $c \in L$ of type $\langle \alpha_1 \ldots \alpha_n s \rangle$ the formula

$$\forall x_1 \ldots x_n\,((Ex_{\sigma_1}i \wedge \ldots \wedge Ex_{\sigma_m}i) \rightarrow cx_1 \ldots x_n i = cx_1 \ldots x_n j),$$

where $\{x_{\sigma_1}, \ldots, x_{\sigma_m}\}$ is the set of all type e variables in $\{x_1, \ldots, x_n\}$. By way of an example, here are the formulae of the above form connected with the constants *walk* and *try*.

$$\forall x\,(Exi \rightarrow walk\,xi = walk\,xj)$$

$$\forall P \forall x\,(Exi \rightarrow try\,Pxi = try\,Pxj).$$

Now define Ξ to be the finite conjunction of all formula obtained in this way (for all $c \in L$) and let $\subseteq$ be a constant of type $\langle ss \rangle$. The following axiom says that $i \subseteq j$ means that i is included in j.

AX11 $\forall ij\,(i \subseteq j = \Xi)$.

Note that $\forall x\,(Exi \to Exi = Exj)$, or, equivalently, $\forall x\,(Exi \to Exj)$ is a conjunct of Ξ; so $i \subseteq j$ implies that the domain of i is contained in that of j. We also have ensured now that sentences like 'John walks' and 'John tries to walk' are true (false) at i if and only if they are true (false) at j, if $i \subseteq j$ and if John exists at i. Let us call this property $\subseteq$-*persistence*. In fact all sentences in our fragment, except those containing the determiners every, a or the are $\subseteq$-persistent.

Theorem 12 *($\subseteq$-Persistency Theorem) If ϑ is an analysis tree of category S that does not contain* every, a *or* the *and if δ_1, ..., δ_n are the free variables and constants of type e occurring in ϑ° then ϑ° $\subseteq$-persists:*

$$\mathrm{AX} \models \forall ij\,(i \subseteq j \wedge E\delta_1 i \wedge \ldots \wedge E\delta_n i \to (\vartheta^\circ i = \vartheta^\circ j)).$$

Here as well as in the rest of this book AX stands for the set of all axioms. For the proof we refer the reader to the Appendix as usual.

What about sentences containing every, a or the, like (20)-(22) above? It seems reasonable to restrict quantification at any index to the denotation of the existence predicate E at that index by redefining the translations of these determiners as follows.

$$\begin{aligned}
\mathsf{every}^\circ &= \lambda P_1 \lambda P_2 \lambda i \forall x\,(Exi \to (P_1 xi \to P_2 xi)) \\
\mathsf{a}^\circ &= \lambda P_1 \lambda P_2 \lambda i \exists x\,(Exi \wedge P_1 xi \wedge P_2 xi) \\
\mathsf{the}^\circ &= \lambda P_1 \lambda P_2 \lambda i \exists x\,(\forall y\,((Eyi \wedge P_1 yi) \leftrightarrow x = y) \wedge P_2 xi)
\end{aligned}$$

The result is that the new translation of (20) will be true in an index i if Mary exists in i and if it is true in some index j such that $i \subseteq j$; it will be false in j if it is false in i in these circumstances. Conversely, (21) retains truth under growth of domain and falsity under shrinkage of domains. But (22) has neither of these properties; it may lose truth as well as falsity both if the domain grows and if the opposite happens.

This explains the intuitions concerning quantified sentences discussed above and it shows that these intuitions do not endanger the conclusion that all sentences in the PTQ fragment of English are $\leq$-persistent. We have these intuitions because quantified sentences fail to be $\subseteq$-persistent, not because they are not $\leq$-persistent.

But it would be rash to conclude that all sentences in natural language are $\leq$-persistent. Veltman 1985 gives examples of expressions that do not seem to be. This author considers two 'information states' the first of which is part of the second:

Information state 1. You are presented with two little boxes, box 1 and box 2. The boxes are closed but you know that together they contain three marbles, a blue one, a yellow one, and a red one, and that each box contains at least one of them.

Information state 2. As 1, except that in addition you know that the blue marble is in box 1. Where the other two marbles are remains a secret.

He then considers sentences of the following kind.

(A) The blue marble may be in box 2
(B) If the yellow marble is in box 1, the red one is in box 2

Clearly, (A) is *true* in the first situation, but *false* in the second; (B) on the other hand is *false* in information state 1, but *true* in information state 2. Hence it seems that (A) and (B) are examples of sentences that are not $\leq$-persistent (not *stable* in Veltman's terminology).

Veltman deals with these instability phenomena in a semantical framework called *Data Semantics* (see also Landman 1986). I shall sketchily introduce the main ideas here (for full information see the works mentioned).

The syntax of Veltman's system is that of ordinary propositional logic enriched with modal operators (*may*, *must*) and a conditional. In order to interpret this logic information models are considered. These are triples $\langle S, \leq, V \rangle$ such that

   (i) $S \neq \emptyset$,
   (ii) $\leq$ partially orders S
   (iii) V is a function with domain S; for each $s \in S$, $V(s)$, written V_s, is a partial function assigning at most one of the values 1 or 0 to atomic sentences. If $s \leq s'$ then $V_s \subseteq V_{s'}$.

In short, information models are defined just like Kripke models for intuitionistic logic, except that on the latter the functions V_s are total.

The next step is to define truth and falsity conditions for sentences on these information models. The relations $s \models_M \varphi$ (meaning that the sentence φ is true in the information model $M = \langle S, \leq, V \rangle$ on the basis of $s \in S$) and $s \dashv_M \varphi$ (φ is false in M on the basis of s) are defined inductively. We show some of the main clauses (suppressing subscripts).

- If φ is atomic, then
  $s \models \varphi \Leftrightarrow V_s(\varphi) = 1$
  $s \dashv \varphi \Leftrightarrow V_s(\varphi) = 0$
- $s \models may\, \varphi \Leftrightarrow$ for some $s' \geq s$, $s' \models \varphi$
  $s \dashv may\, \varphi \Leftrightarrow$ for no $s' \geq s$, $s' \models \varphi$
- $s \models if\, \varphi\, then\, \psi \Leftrightarrow$ for no $s' \geq s$, $s' \models \varphi$ and $s' \dashv \psi$
  $s \dashv if\, \varphi\, then\, \psi \Leftrightarrow$ for some $s' \geq s$, $s' \models \varphi$ and $s' \dashv \psi$.

The propositional connectives $\neg$, $\wedge$ and $\vee$ are evaluated according to the Strong Kleene evaluation scheme.

It is easy to show now that sentences of the form $may\, p$ can be true in some information state while being false in a state extending it. Similarly, it is easy to find an information model such that *if p then q* is false in one state but true in another of which the first one is a part. Thus the instability phenomena are explained in Data Semantics.

We can do very much the same thing in our framework. For the moment let us work with the three-valued variant TT_2^3 of our logic, as Veltman's system is three-valued too. Truth and falsity conditions for conditionals and modals equal to Veltman's can then be obtained by translating as follows.

$$\text{if}^\circ \ = \ \lambda p \lambda q \lambda i \, (\exists j \, (j \geq i \wedge pj \wedge \neg qj) \neq \top)$$
$$\text{maybe}^\circ \ = \ \lambda p \lambda i \, (\exists j \, (j \geq i \wedge pj) = \top)$$

Sentences like If John walks Mary talks and Maybe John walks are now treated in a way completely analogous to the way they are dealt with in Data Semantics and are not $\leq$-persistent.

The translations here may not automatically carry over to the four-valued variant of type logic. It is questionable whether we want Maybe John walks to be true in a coherent situation if there are only *incoherent* situations extending it in which John walks. Similarly, we may not want If John walks Mary talks to be false in a coherent situation simply because there is an incoherent situation extending it where John walks but Mary does not talk. It seems that the most natural way to extend these analyses to TT_2^4 is to restrict the existential quantifications in the translations of if and maybe to the *coherent* extensions of the index i. If a conditional sentence or a sentence expressing epistemic possibility is then evaluated in a coherent situation such as the actual world, only its coherent extensions contribute to the truth value of the sentence.

Strong consequence and weak consequence

The first thing to note when we look at the logic that the verb believe receives in our new system is that we have achieved what we have set out to achieve in the Introduction: the inference from sentence (3) to sentence (4) is blocked. (For ease of reference sentences (1)–(4) are repeated below.) We can now easily find a partial model such that the translation of (1), *walk john*, is true at some index while the translation of (2), $\lambda i \, (walk \ john \ i \wedge (talk \ bill \ i \vee \neg talk \ bill \ i))$, is undefined at that index. The inference from (1) to (2) is blocked for the reason that it is irrelevant. As a consequence the unwanted inference from (3) to (4) is invalid too.

(1) John walks
(2) John walks and Bill talks or Bill does not talk
(3) Mary believes that John walks
(4) Mary believes that John walks and Bill talks or Bill does not talk

Now one may find that the price that was paid for blocking the unwanted entailments has been somewhat high. Did we really want to cut out the inference from (1) to (2) as well as the one from (3) to (4)? It may be true that in a strong sense of the word (2) does not follow from (1) since the converse inference is valid and the two sentences are not strictly synonymous, but certainly there is a weaker sense in which the entailment, although irrelevant, nevertheless seems unobjectionable: If (1) is true, true in the real world, then (2) is true as well and if (2) is actually false then (1) is so too.

This is an instance of a more general problem. Let us consider the conditions under which substitution of one expression for another is allowed *salva veritate* in natural language. The rules that govern the acceptability of such substitutions seem to be highly dependent on context. If the expression that is to be substituted occurs in the context of a sentence complement taking verbs such as believe or know the rules are rather strict while they are much looser if the expression is not in such a context. Possible world semantics has solved part of the riddle what the substitutability rules are, it explains e.g. why substituting 'Ed' for 'the Mayor of Amsterdam' in 'Mary believes the Mayor of Amsterdam to be a clever man' is not guaranteed to preserve truth even if Ed happens to be the Mayor. But there are residual problems for it seems that even expressions that are usually treated as equivalent in possible world semantics are not interchangeable in these contexts. The sentences given above form an example, but there are more. For example, while it is generally accepted that the expressions 'doctor' and 'physician' are equivalent in meaning, these words are not interchangeable in all contexts as we shall argue in Chapter 9. Other examples can be obtained with the help of simple arithmetical statements: (23) and (24) may differ in truth value while the embedded expressions are both taken to be true in all possible worlds.

(23) Mary believes that $2 + 3 = 5$

(24) Mary believes that $3489 + 2275 = 5764$

Clearly, if we wish to retain the commitment to Leibniz's Law we expressed in Chapter 3 we cannot treat these non-interchangeable pairs of expressions as if they were equivalent. Just as we have found a semantics that treats (1) and (2) differently we are committed to finding a way of treating the pairs 'doctor' and 'physician' and '$2 + 3 = 5$' and '$3489 + 2275 = 5764$' as non-equivalent. But as soon as we succeed in taking this step a new problem threatens, for while we shall then have succeeded to explain why the pairs in question are not interchangeable in intensional contexts, we shall no longer be able to explain why the expressions can be substituted one for the other outside of these contexts.

There is a very simple solution to this problem however. In order to show how it works let me first formalize our strong notion of entailment, the one that blocks substitution of sentence (1) for sentence (2) in all contexts. After that we can define a weaker relation of consequence from it, a relation that does not permit intersubstitution of (1) and (2) in intensional contexts but allows it outside of these contexts.

We say that a model is *intended* if it satisfies all the axioms in AX. If Γ and Δ are sets of terms of type $\langle \alpha_1 \ldots \alpha_n \rangle$, then we write $\Gamma \models_{AX} \Delta$ for $\Gamma, \{\lambda x_{\alpha_1} \ldots \lambda x_{\alpha_n} \varphi \mid \varphi \in AX\} \models \Delta$. Since we shall take care to have only bivalent sentences (sentences that are either true and not false or false and not true in any model) as axioms, this gives a notion of logical consequence that takes only intended models into account: $\Gamma \models_{AX} \Delta$ if and only if in each intended model the partial intersection of the values of the terms in Γ is partially included in the partial union of the values of the terms in Δ. An analysis tree ϑ of any category is said to *follow strongly* from a set of trees Ξ of that category if $\Xi^\circ \models_{AX} \varphi^\circ$. Analysis trees ξ and ϑ are called *strongly synonymous* if ξ strongly follows from ϑ and ϑ strongly follows from ξ.

Note that if Γ and Δ consist of terms of some type ending in s we can alternatively describe $\Gamma \models_{AX} \Delta$ as: in each intended model and in each situation i in that model the partial intersection of the extensions of the terms in Γ in i is partially included in the partial union of the extensions of the terms in Δ in i. This suggests that we can weaken this notion of entailment by imposing constraints on the kind of situations at which evaluation can take place. One way to impose such constraints is of course to give more axioms of the kind that we have been using freely thus far. But note that axioms of the sentential type $\langle \rangle$ are bound to have a *global* effect: the constraints they impose on one situation they impose on all. There is a subtler way to impose constraints: instead of axioms of type $\langle \rangle$ we can use terms of propositional type (type $\langle s \rangle$) to put restrictions on situations. The restricting terms will then have the same type as our translations of natural language sentences have. Let MP be a set of such type $\langle s \rangle$ meaning postulates (we shall specify MP as the set $\{MP1, \ldots, MP6\}$ below) and let us say that an analysis tree ϑ of any category A such that $\tau(A) = \langle \alpha_1 \ldots \alpha_n s \rangle$ *weakly follows* from a set of trees Ξ of that category if it holds that $\Xi^\circ, \{\lambda x_{\alpha_1} \ldots \lambda x_{\alpha_n} \Phi \mid \Phi \in MP\} \models_{AX} \vartheta^\circ$. That is, a tree ϑ weakly follows from a tree ξ if and only if in each intended model, in each situation i in that model satisfying the meaning postulates, the extension of ξ° in i is partially included in the extension of ϑ° in i. Analysis trees ξ and ϑ are called *weakly synonymous* if ξ weakly follows from ϑ and ϑ weakly follows from ξ.

We shall use weak entailment as our explication of the relation of entailment in natural language.

To see how this works, let Ω be the conjunction of all formulae of the form $\forall x_1 \ldots x_n (cx_1 \ldots x_n i = \top \vee cx_1 \ldots x_n i = \bot)$, where $c \in L$ and i is some fixed type s variable. The formula Ω thus says that i is a *world*, a total and coherent situation, a situation in which everything is defined and nothing is overdefined. Now let's restrict evaluation to the set of worlds, specifying our first meaning postulate as follows.

MP1 $\lambda i \, \Omega$

Note that, as an immediate consequence of this meaning postulate, sentences (1) and (2) are weakly synonymous. Clearly there is no world where these sentences differ in truth value. But weak synonymy is no sufficient condition for interchangeability in belief contexts: sentences (3) and (4) may still have different truth values. Only strong synonymy warrants interchangeability. The extra premise, $\lambda i \, \Omega$, whose meaning we can informally describe as 'The present index is total and coherent', has a purely local effect. It will give a coarse-grained semantics to sentences that have no intensional expressions occurring in them, but it will have no effect on the logic of those expressions that occur within the scope of an intensional operator.

This suggests a general way to strengthen substitutability conditions in intensional contexts: First strengthen the relation of entailment globally, then make reparations on the local level with the help of meaning postulates, such that the net effect on the logic on the local level, outside of any intensional context, is nil. In Chapter 9 we shall use this method to obtain what we hope are the right substitutability conditions for pairs such as 'doctor' and 'physician' and 'lawyer' and 'attorney' and a similar strategy can be used to solve some of the problems with sentences containing arithmetical statements. Surely one could enforce that arithmetical expressions such as $3489 + 2275 = 5764$ come out true in all possible situations by stipulating that (some index-relativized version of) the second order Peano Axioms holds in all of them. But this would have the wrong result that true (false) arithmetical expressions would be predicted to be interchangeable with other true (false) arithmetical expressions everywhere. In particular (23) and (24) would be predicted to be equivalent, which they are not. As an alternative one could adopt meaning postulates to the effect that the natural numbers obey the Peano Axioms *at the present index* (these meaning postulates, then, would be of the form $\lambda i \, \varphi$ where φ is one of the index-relativized Peano Axioms). This would predict arithmetical statements having the same truth values to be equivalent but it would block their interchangeability in opaque contexts. I shall not work this out in detail, but the principle is clear.

In this book we take the position that the logic of the natural language connectives and, or and not is the strong (relevant) logic described in Chapter 5. This means that sentences that are propositionally equivalent on the basis of this logic are predicted to be mutually substitutable, disregarding the context in which they occur. But note that our way of doing things does not commit us to imposing this particular logic on the natural language connectives. It would be easy to block *all* entailments arising from these connectives by simply changing the translation function ∘ slightly: wherever ∧, ∨ or ¬ appears in the present translation replace it by a *non*-logical constant *and*, *or* or *not* (of types $\langle\langle s\rangle\langle s\rangle s\rangle$, $\langle\langle s\rangle\langle s\rangle s\rangle$ and $\langle\langle s\rangle s\rangle$ respectively) in the way suggested by the following examples.

$$([\xi\vartheta]^{11a})^\circ = and\ \xi^\circ\vartheta^\circ;$$
$$([\xi\vartheta]^{13})^\circ = \lambda P\,(or\,(\xi^\circ P)(\vartheta^\circ P));$$
$$([\xi\vartheta]^{17a})^\circ = not\ \xi^\circ\vartheta^\circ.$$

Clearly this would ruin all entailments that are based on the relevant logic of ∧, ∨ and ¬. But it would be possible to re-obtain classical logic locally by accepting the following as meaning postulates.

$$\lambda i \forall p \forall q \,(and\ pqi = pi \wedge qi)$$
$$\lambda i \forall p \forall q \,(or\ pqi = pi \vee qi)$$
$$\lambda i \forall p \,(not\ pi = \neg pi)$$

Similar moves with respect to the quantifiers would get us a relation of logical consequence that is completely classical outside intensional contexts but that is such that the relation of interchangeability in arbitrary contexts is virtually coextensive with the relation of syntactical identity. This last notion of entailment is usually associated with a treatment of the attitudes as relations between persons and syntactic entities and is usually considered too fine-grained. We see here that even this extremely fine granularity is consistent with the approach that treats attitudes as relations between persons and propositions.[3] Of course the most coarse-grained notion of entailment, classical equivalence, is available in this approach as well. Between these two extremes a whole gamut of possibilities exists, of which our official notion of weak consequence is only one. The reader who prefers one of these possibilities to our official one is invited to take his choice.

---

[3]See Muskens 1991b for a maximally fine-grained treatment of meaning in relation with the problem of 'logical omniscience' on the basis of classical logic.

8

Propositional Attitudes

In this chapter we shall use our framework of partialized Montague Grammar to give a treatment of the propositional attitude verbs—neutral perception verbs included—along the lines of Barwise 1981 and Barwise and Perry 1983 (B&P). Our main object is to show that, now that we have the basic ontology of Situation Semantics (situations, the part-of relation, persistence) at our disposal, we can carry out specific analyses of natural language phenomena that were given in that theory in a rather compact and parsimonious way. We shall mainly be concerned with finding the right translations for the verbs in question and with constraining the class of models by appropriate axioms and meaning postulates.

Belief, doubt, knowledge and assertion

In the previous chapter we have been able to get rid of certain unwanted substitutions in epistemic contexts, but our treatment of expressions involving the verbs believe and know still is not quite right. The failure is on the positive side this time: there are types of entailment that we do want but that are not treated as valid by our analysis thus far.[1] For example, it is arguable that (26) and (27) should both follow from (25) (this type of

---

[1] On the other hand it might be argued that even the present analysis allows for too many substitutions in epistemic contexts, as expressions which are strongly synonymous can still be substituted for one another *salva veritate*. A more extreme view on epistemic contexts would allow no entailment under a belief operator at all, i.e. would never allow one to logically infer Mary believes that A from Mary believes that B unless A is syntactically identical to B. It seems that this is the only view on the attitudes which avoids problems of 'logical omniscience' of any kind. Once this position is taken it must of course be explained why some inferences seem valid nevertheless, e.g. why (30) seems to follow from (26) and (29); but it could be argued that the latter inference is no instance of a *logically* valid argument but that we are just willing to accept (30) once we have accepted (26) and (29) because we are inclined to ascribe certain logical faculties to agents, although we do not think they are logically omniscient. In Muskens 1991b I have worked out this view and have shown that, despite appearances, it can be formalized with the help of classical type logic. The approach that is followed here is in conformity with the intuitions about entailments that we find in B&P.

entailment is called *Conjunction Distribution*), but on the account given
they do not. Similarly, (28) should follow from (26) as well as from (27);
(25) should follow from the conjunction of (26) and (27); and (26) plus (29)
should have (30) as a consequence (the latter type of entailment is called
Weak Substitution).

(25) Mary believes that John walks and Bill talks

(26) Mary believes that Bill talks

(27) Mary believes that John walks

(28) Mary believes that John walks or Bill talks

(29) Mary believes that Bill is a man

(30) Mary believes that a man talks

We can get a theory of belief sentences that predicts this behaviour by
following classical Situation Semantics very closely and treating the expression believe that in Hintikka's way. To this end we have introduced a
constant B of type $\langle ess \rangle$ into our language L. The informal interpretation
of a formula of the form $Bxji$ is that in situation i situation j is classified
as compatible with x's beliefs. Since B is a partial relation like any other,
the classification need not be total: there may be situations j that are
neither classified as compatible nor as incompatible with x's beliefs at i.
Nor need the relation be coherent: some indices may be counted both as
compatible and as incompatible with x's beliefs at i—if i is incoherent. We
call a situation j a *doxastic option* of x in i if $Bxij$ is true in the model
under consideration and we call it a *doxastic alternative* of x in i if $Bxij$
is not false. So, a situation is a doxastic alternative of x in i if and only
if it is in the complement of the antidenotation of $\lambda j\, Bxji$. Of course, if
i is a world, a total and coherent situation, then a situation is a doxastic
alternative of a given person if and only if it is one of his doxastic options.

Now, writing $T\varphi$ ('φ is true') for $(\varphi = \top) \vee (\varphi = \#)$, redefine the
translation of believe that as follows:

$$\text{believe that}^{\circ} = \lambda p \lambda x \lambda i \forall j\, (Bxji \to Tpj)$$

The resulting Hintikka analysis of belief sentences is equivalent to the analysis of these expressions given in B&P. For example, the translation of sen-
tence (26), $\lambda i \forall j\, (B\,mary\,ji \to T\,walk\ bill\,j)$, will be true at some index i
just if Bill walks at all Mary's doxastic alternatives in i; it will be false at
index i just if Bill does not walk at some of Mary's doxastic options there.

Belief is now no longer merely closed under substitution of strong synonyms; it is closed under strong consequence as well: if a person believes
that A and B follows strongly from A or if he believes that A_1 and at the
same time believes that A_2 and B follows strongly from A_1 and A_2, then it
follows that the person believes that B. Hence the entailments cited above
come out valid: they are all of this type.

The treatment will work for other propositional attitudes too, provided that we make the necessary modifications in each case. Here are some extra translations:

$$\text{assert that}^\circ = \lambda p \lambda x \lambda i \forall j \, (Axji \to Tpj)$$
$$\text{know that}^\circ = \lambda p \lambda x \lambda i \forall j \, (Kxji \to Tpj)$$
$$\text{doubt that}^\circ = \lambda p \lambda x \lambda i \exists j \, (Bxji \land \neg Tpj)$$

The expression assert that is treated just like believe that, except that in its translation the relation B is replaced by a relation A of the same type. The denotation of $\lambda j \, Axji$ consists of those situations j in which that what is asserted by x in i is not false; its antidenotation is formed by those indices in which that what is asserted by x in i is not true. The expression know that is dealt with in the same way; Mary knows that John walks is true if and only if it is true that John walks in all Mary's epistemic alternatives, false if it is not true that John walks at one of her epistemic options. The translation of doubt that is chosen in a way that will ensure that e.g. sentences (31) and (32) are equivalent. Conjunction Distribution fails here: for example (32) does not follow from (34) under this analysis. Both (32) and (33) can on the other hand be inferred from sentence (35), this type of entailment is called *Disjunction Distribution*.

(31) Mary does not believe that John walks

(32) Mary doubts that John walks

(33) Mary doubts that Bill talks

(34) Mary doubts that John walks and Bill talks

(35) Mary doubts that John walks or Bill talks

(36) Mary knows that John walks

(37) Mary knows that John does not walk

(38) Mary does not know that John walks

(39) Mary believes that John does not walk

(40) Mary does not believe that John walks

(41) Mary believes that John walks and John does not walk

(42) Mary believes that John talks and John does not talk

(43) Mary knows that she knows that John walks

We have given the translations of believe that, know that and assert that all the same form, let us now pay attention to some of the differences in logical behaviour between these expressions. For example, unlike the other two verbs know that is a *factive*: if somebody knows that φ, then φ. To get this right, we let AX12 be an axiom. Any agent in any situation will find that situation itself among his epistemic options as well as among his epistemic alternatives. This will ensure for example that John walks follows (weakly) from sentence (36) (*Veridicality* or *Factivity*); it will also ensure that (38) is weakly entailed by (37) (*Negation*). We do not predict this last type of entailment to obtain for belief sentences: (40) does not follow from (39). I think this is correct, since people are far from rational in their beliefs and may easily believe (classical) contradictions. Note, by the way, that belief in one contradiction does not entail belief in arbitrary other contradictions: (42) does not follow from (41). Readers who believe that *Negation* holds for belief sentences and believe that both (41) and (42) are contradictory, may want to impose the constraint that everybody has at least one coherent situation among his doxastic options.

Axioms AX13 and AX14, in which the double-headed arrow of Chapter 5 is put to use, stipulate that both the denotations and the complements of the antidenotations of the accessibility relations $\lambda ij\, Kxji$ and $\lambda ij\, Bxji$ (for given x) are transitive. To know implies to know that one knows and (43) now follows from (36). A similar type of entailment is valid for believe, but fails for assert: if you believe something then you believe that you believe it, but you can assert something without asserting that you did.

AX15 says that an agent's doxastic options are among his epistemic options and that any of his doxastic alternatives is one of his epistemic alternatives as well. This enforces that sentence (36) entails sentence (27) and in general that knowledge involves belief.

AX12 $\forall x \forall i\, (Kxii = \top)$

AX13 $\forall x \forall ijk\, ((Kxji \wedge Kxkj) \twoheadrightarrow Kxki))$

AX14 $\forall x \forall ijk\, ((Bxji \wedge Bxkj) \twoheadrightarrow Bxki))$

AX15 $\forall x \forall ij\, (Bxji \twoheadrightarrow Kxji)$

Neutral perception

Now I turn to the treatment of the neutral perception verb see. Although I shall treat this expression as a verb that takes sentential complements and that forms intransitive verb phrases with these, I shall not assign it to the same category IV/S that the other attitude verbs are assigned to. Instead, we list it as an expression of category $IV//S$. To the definition of analysis tree we add an extra clause which runs as follows.

G18. If $x \in AT_{IV//S}$ and $\vartheta \in AT_S$, then $[\xi\vartheta]^{18} \in AT_{IV}$.

The definition of the translation function ∘ must also get an extra clause; treating G18 as an ordinary application rule, we define:

T18. $([\xi\vartheta]^{18})^\circ = \xi^\circ \vartheta^\circ$

Following B&P again we shall say that a sentence of the form a sees φ (where a is a noun phrase and φ is an embedded uninflected sentence) is true in a situation i just in case it is true that a sees some situation in which j is true; a sees φ is false if it is false that a sees any situation or if in a's visual scene (a is supposed to see at most one scene) the embedded sentence φ is not true. In other words, we choose the following translation for the new lexical element see (where see xji is to be read as: 'x sees j in i'):

$$\text{see}° = \lambda p \lambda x \lambda i \exists j \, (see \, xji \wedge Tpj).$$

Some constraints must be imposed; the first is that a person can only see maximally one scene at a time.

MP2 $\lambda i \forall x \forall j k \, ((see \, xji \wedge see \, xki) \rightarrow j = k)$

The second constraint involves the relation between a visual scene and the situation in which it is seen; the former is part of a situation that is included in the latter.

MP3 $\lambda i \forall x \forall j \, (see \, xji \rightarrow \exists k \, (k \subseteq i \wedge j \leq k))$

This analysis works well enough, as long as the embedded sentences do not contain any determiners (for that case see below). First note that our treatment of the irrelevant entailments in the case of the epistemic and doxastic attitudes carries over to the attitudes of perception without any difficulty: Sentences (5) and (6) are not synonymous, not even weakly so. Second, our theory predicts the same entailment phenomena as the B&P theory does. For example, from MP3 and the fact that all determiner-free sentences $\subseteq$-persist we see that sentence (5) weakly entails its embedded sentence John walks (*Veridicality*). In a similar way we see that (46) follows weakly from (45) (*Negation*). MP2 assures us that (5) and (44) entail (47) (see Barwise 1981 for a discussion of this type of entailment). We also have logical principles like *Conjunction Distribution* and *Disjunction Distribution*: for example (47) entails (48) and (50) follows from (49).

(5)   Mary sees John walk

(6)   Mary sees John walk and Bill talk or Bill not talk

(44) Mary sees Bill talk

(45) Mary sees John not walk

(46) Mary does not see John walk

(47) Mary sees John walk and Bill talk

(48) Mary sees John walk and Mary sees Bill talk

(49) Mary sees John walk or Bill talk

(50) Mary sees John walk or Mary sees Bill talk

To make the treatment work for arbitrary sentences of the fragment, including those that have a determiner occurring in the complement of a neutral perception verb, some extra care must be taken. Consider sentence (51). According to our analysis thus far, but contrary to intuition, this sentence is ambiguous. It has a *de re* reading, given in (51a), in which the noun phrase a man takes scope over the perception verb see, as well as a de dicto reading, given in (51b), in which see has scope over a man. A similar remark can be made about sentences (52)–(54): each has a reading (given in (52a), (53a) and (54a) respectively) obtained by 'quantifying-in' as well as a reading (given in (52b), (53b) and (54b)), that can be got by more direct means.

(51) Mary sees a man walk

a $[[\text{a man}]^3[\text{Mary [see [he}_0\text{ walk}]^4]^{18}]^4]^{14,0}$
$\lambda i \exists x \,(Exi \wedge man\, xi \wedge \exists j\,(see\ mary\,ji \wedge T\,walk\,xj))$

b $*[\text{Mary [see [[a man}]^3\text{ walk}]^4]^{18}]^4$
$\lambda i \exists j\,(see\ mary\,ji \wedge T\exists x\,(Exj \wedge man\,xj \wedge walk\,xj))$

(52) Mary sees the man walk

a $[[\text{the man}]^3[\text{Mary [see [he}_0\text{ walk}]^4]^{18}]^4]^{14,0}$
$\lambda i \exists x \,(\forall y\,((Eyi \wedge man\,yi) \leftrightarrow x = y) \wedge \exists j\,(see\ mary\,ji \wedge$
$T\,walk\,xj)$

b $*[\text{Mary [see [[the man}]^3\text{ walk}]^4]^{18}]^4$
$\lambda i \exists j\,(see\ mary\,ji \wedge T\exists x\,(\forall y\,((Eyj \wedge man\,yj) \leftrightarrow x = y) \wedge$
$walk\,xj))$

(53) Mary sees every man walk

a $[[\text{every man}]^3\,[\text{Mary [see [he}_0\text{ walk}]^4]^{18}]^4]^{14,0}$
$\lambda i \forall x \,(Exi \wedge man\,xi) \rightarrow \exists j\,(see\ mary\,ji \wedge T\,walk\,xj))$

b $*[\text{Mary [see [[every man}]^3\text{ walk}]^4]^{18}]^4$
$\lambda i \exists j\,(see\ mary\,ji \wedge T\forall x\,((Exj \wedge man\,xj) \rightarrow walk\,xj))$

(54) Mary sees no man walk

a $[[\text{no man}]^3\,[\text{Mary [see [he}_0\text{ walk}]^4]^{18}]^4]^{14,0}$
$\lambda i \neg\exists x \,(Exi \wedge man\,xi \wedge \exists j\,(see\ mary\,ji \wedge T\,walk\,xj)$

b $*[\text{Mary [see [[no man}]^3\text{ walk}]^4]^{18}]^4$
$\lambda i \exists j\,(see\ mary\,ji \wedge T\neg\exists x\,(Exj \wedge man\,xj \wedge walk\,xj))$

Looking at the semantics of these sentences we see that in each case the *de re* but not the *de dicto* readings give the right truth conditions. Consider a case in which Mary sees Bill walk. Bill is a man, but he is too far away to enable Mary to see this. Then (51) is true, but (51b) could be false since Bill is not in the positive extension of the predicate 'man' at Mary's visual scene. Similarly, we can easily imagine situations in which the truth values of (52b), (53b) and (54b) differ from the intuitive semantics of sentences (52), (53) and (54), the expressions they are supposed to formalize respectively.

Note that we cannot characterize the correct readings by simply stipulating that neutral perception verbs may not take scope over determiners. In (55a) for example, a perfectly acceptable non-specific reading of sentence (55), the verb see has scope over the determiner a. Sentence (55) has a correct specific reading (55b) as well, in which a pen takes scope over both see and seek. But the intermediate reading (55c), that has a pen taking scope over seek, while see has scope over a pen, is out: There is no natural reading of (55) that implies the existence of a pen in Mary's visual field.

(55) Mary sees Bill seek a pen

    a [Mary [see [Bill [seek [a pen]^3]^5]^4]^{18}]^4

        $\lambda i \exists j \, (see \; mary \; ji \wedge$

           $T\,try \, (\lambda y \lambda i \exists x \, (Exi \wedge pen \; xi \wedge find \; xyi)) \, bill \; j)$

    b [[a pen]^3 [Mary [see [Bill [seek he$_0$]^5]^4]^{18}]^4]^{14,0}

        $\lambda i \exists x \, (Exi \wedge pen \; xi \wedge \exists j \, (see \; mary \; ji \wedge T\,try \, (find \; x) \, bill \; j)$

    c *[Mary [see [[a pen]^3 [Bill [seek he$_0$]^5]^4]^{14,0}]^{18}]^4

        $\lambda i \exists j \, (see \; mary \; ji \wedge T \exists x \, (Exj \wedge pen \; xj \wedge$

           $try(find \; x) \, bill \; j))$

Then what is it that the bad readings (52b), (53b), (54b) and (55c) have in common but that distinguishes them from the good readings (52a), (53a), (54a), (55a) and (55b)? It is a semantical property: in the translation of each of the bad trees a quantification occurs over the domain of individuals occurring in somebody's visual scene. We must conclude with Asher and Bonevac 1985, Asher and Bonevac 1987 that no such quantification is allowed. Quantifiers are not interpreted in scenes. In normal situations the domain of objects associated with a person's field of vision changes rapidly over time; even the tiniest movement of the eye can cause objects to be introduced into ones domain of vision and can cause other objects to be expelled from it. It seems that language users are therefore extremely reluctant to interpret expressions that are not $\subseteq$-persistent in their visual fields.

Formally we can characterize the good readings by adopting the following definition.[2]

Definition 48 An analysis tree is called *admissible* if for all its subtrees of the form $[\xi \vartheta]^{18}$ the term ϑ° is $\subseteq$-persistent.

Meanings are now associated with admissible readings only. For example (55c) is ruled inadmissible and is not associated with a meaning because it has

$$[see \, [[a \; pen]^3 \, [Bill \, [seek \; he_0]^5]^4]^{14,0}]^{18}$$

as a subtree and the translation of

$$[[a \; pen]^3 \, [Bill \, [seek \; he_0]^5]^4]^{14,0},$$

which is

$$\lambda i \exists x \, (Exi \wedge pen \; xi \wedge try(find \; x) \, bill \; i),$$

[2]See Hendriks 1993 for an interesting alternative account of what Hendriks calls 'scope sieves'. Hendriks uses a flexible version of Montague Grammar in order to rule out inadmissable readings of noun phrases in neutral perception contexts.

is not $\subseteq$-persistent. On the other hand, (55a) and (55b) are admissible since both

$$try\,(\lambda y \lambda i \exists x\,(Exi \wedge pen\,xi \wedge find\,xyi))\,bill$$

and the open term $try\,(find\,x)\,bill\,\subseteq$-persist. Similarly, the a-readings in (51)–(54) can be seen to be admissible but the b-readings are out; the verb see takes non-$\subseteq$-persistent complements in them.

(56) A man walks

(57) The man walks

(58) Every man walks

(59) No man walks

(60) Bill seeks a pen

(61) John is the man

(62) John is a man

If we restrict the set of readings thus, the basic facts about entailments involving neutral perception sentences are predicted. The theory gets the Veridicality phenomena right: (56), (57) and (58) follow weakly from (51), (52) and (53) respectively. But of course (59) is not weakly entailed by (54), nor should it be. Notice that (60) follows weakly from (55), or, to be more precise, its *de dicto* reading follows weakly from (55)'s *de dicto* reading (55a) and its *de re* reading is weakly entailed by (55)'s *de re* reading (55b). *Substitutivity* also holds: for example from (5) and (61) sentence (52) follows. Relatedly, we may see that (51) follows from sentences (5) and (62). Lastly, note that the theory predicts the facts about so-called *Exportation* in a trivial way. As was noted in Barwise 1981, the noun phrase a man in (51) can be 'exported' to give it widest possible scope without change of meaning. Thus (51) entails 'There is a man such that Mary sees him walk'. Our theory indeed predicts this; in the translation of (51) the existential quantifier already has widest possible scope. In fact our theory predicts that *all* noun phrases will show this behaviour. This conforms to an observation made in Higginbotham 1983.

9

Names

Daß kein Name mich täuscht,
Daß mich kein Dogma beschränkt ...
Goethe

Given the fact that Hesperus is Phosphorus, why do the sentences 'Hesperus is Hesperus' and 'Hesperus is Phosphorus' differ in cognitive value? This essentially is the puzzle that Frege set to himself in the first pages of his famous *Über Sinn und Bedeutung*. On the last page the question is answered: Although the names 'Hesperus' and 'Phosphorus' refer to the same object (the planet Venus) and hence have the same Bedeutung they nevertheless differ in meaning (*Sinn*). They therefore make different contributions to the meanings of the sentences in which they occur and this explains the fact that the two identity statements are not synonymous, even though they have the same truth value. Since for the cognitive value (*Erkenntniswert*) of a sentence not only its truth value but also its meaning has to be taken into account, this in its turn explains the difference in cognitive value.

Frege's answer to the puzzle has been very popular among the philosophers of the first two-thirds of this century, but during the last decades it has been under heavy attack. Influenced by authors such as Kripke and Donnellan, many philosophers and semanticists nowadays reject the view that coreferential names can differ in meaning. Instead, they accept the following theory, which can be traced back to John Stuart Mill:

(M) The meaning of a proper name depends only on its referent.

The semantical theory given in the preceding chapters may serve as an example of a theory that conforms to principle (M). The meaning of the proper name John, for example, was equated in this theory with the property of being a property of the individual John, the name's actual bearer. This was in accordance with the Montagovian tradition. Now, the property of being a property of an individual thing is of course uniquely determined by that thing itself. So the meaning of John depended only on John.

Whatever merits the Millian theory of names may have, it has one important drawback: it leads almost directly to wrong predictions about the semantics of English. It predicts certain entailments to hold that are flatly refuted by the semantical judgements of those who speak the language. It predicts that certain pairs of sentences, one of which is judged to be false while the other is not, are synonymous. Here is a famous example of such a pair.

(63) The Ancients believed that Hesperus was Phosphorus

(64) The Ancients believed that Hesperus was Hesperus

If the meaning of a proper name depends only on its referent, then, since the names 'Hesperus' and 'Phosphorus' name the same thing, they must mean the same as well. But if they have the same meaning (if they are synonymous) they will make the same contributions to the meanings of the sentences in which they occur and in particular the second occurrence of 'Hesperus' in (64) and the only occurrence of 'Phosphorus' in (63) will make the same contributions to the meanings of these sentences respectively. Hence the two sentences must be synonymous. But clearly they are not, since the first one is false while the second is not. It seems that our initial assumption was incorrect and that there is more to the meaning of a name than just its reference.

In this Chapter we shall first analyze the Fregean argument against (M) a bit further and we shall see that it rests on certain minimal assumptions which are at the heart of empirical semantics. We shall also consider Kripke's attempts to refute the argument or at least to cast doubt on its acceptability, but the conclusion will be reached that the argument cannot be circumvented if we are to respect our fundamental minimal assumptions. In a second section we shall then reconsider Frege's and Russell's theory that names are descriptions, formalize a weak version of that theory, and defend it against certain objections that were made against it by Kripke and others.

The Millian theory of names

Let us consider the premises on which Frege's argument against (M) rests. Apart from the assumption that the Millian theory is correct, the assumption that was to be refuted, we used another premise in this *reductio*. This premise is widely known as *Frege's Principle* and we formulate it thus:

(L) *Synonyms are intersubstitutable without change in meaning.*

That is, if B is any expression of any linguistic category, then replacing any of its parts A by a synonym A' will result in an expression B' that is synonymous with the original B.

Frege's Principle is closely related to the principle of *Compositionality*:

(C) *The meaning of a complex expression is a function of the meanings of its direct parts.*

Under some very natural and very weak assumptions about the *direct part* relation between expressions of natural language, it can be shown that principle (L) follows from principle (C).[1]

The converse is true as well, but only if we allow the meanings of complex expressions to be determined by *arbitrary* functions; if we make the additional but very natural demand that these functions be *computable* the two principles are no longer equivalent.

Principle (L) seems to hold a priori. This is best seen if, by contraposition, we assume that we are confronted with two nonsynonymous expressions such that one results from substituting one of the other's parts A by an expression A' of the same category. In a case like this we must surely conclude that A and A' are different in meaning. What else could cause the nonsynonymy of the original pair of expressions? It seems part of the meaning of 'meaning' that A and A' are not synonymous in this case.

But the strongest reason for accepting Frege's Principle is not that it seems to hold *a priori* for the concept of meaning, nor that it follows from the theoretically fruitful and widely accepted principle of Compositionality. The best reason to accept it is that it is an instance of Leibniz's Law since it has the following form:

$$A = B \rightarrow [A/x]C = [B/x]C.$$

Identity is synonymy, identity of meaning, in the theory of meaning, and there is no reason to assume that in the theory of meaning the notion of identity should not be subjected to the ordinary identity axioms. Every

---

[1]Let the relation of being a *proper part* be defined as the transitive closure of the direct part relation and let the relation of being a *part* be its transitive reflexive closure. Then A is a proper part of B if and only if it is a part of one of its direct parts. The assumptions that we need are (a) that no expression is one of its own proper parts and (b) that no expression has more than a finite number of proper parts. In other words, we must make the very natural assumption that the direct part relation is a finite directed acyclic graph. Now let B' result from B by replacing one of its parts A by a synonym A'. We prove by induction on the number of B's proper parts that B and B' are synonymous. This is trivial if A is B itself, so let A be one of B's proper parts and hence a part of one of its direct parts C. Then B' is the result of replacing C by C' in B, where C' is the result of replacing A by A' in C. Since C is not a proper part of itself and all of C's proper parts are also proper parts of B, C has less proper parts than B has and by the induction hypothesis we see that C and C' have the same meaning. But then B and B' must have the same meaning too since the meaning of a complex expression is a function of the meanings of its direct parts.

theory has its basic relation of congruence; in set theory this relation is 'having the same elements'; in model theory it is isomorphism; in topology it is homeomorphism; in phonetics it is 'being the same sound'; in English phonology it is 'belonging to the same phoneme of English'; in semantics it is synonymy. Viewed in this light (L) is not just another attractive principle that we might or might not choose to accept, in the way it seems that we may or may not accept the nice building block picture of meaning that Compositionality has to offer, it is the *sine qua non* of semantics.

But (L) by itself is not strong enough to refute the Millian assumption; in fact on its own it cannot discriminate between any two meanings. For instance, strictly speaking it is quite compatible with the principle that *all* expressions that belong to the same category be synonymous. Of course, although this perversity is compatible with (L), it is not compatible with our intuitive judgements about language. The following principle of observational adequacy takes these judgements into account.

(O) *If ordinary speakers judge that two sentences may differ in truth value, then these sentences are not synonymous.*

While I take it that Leibniz's Law (L) is essential to semantics if semantics is to be a *formal* theory, principle (O) is to be accepted if we want semantics to be an *empirical* discipline; acceptance of (O) makes us leave the realm of pure philosophy and enter that of linguistics.

Now let us restate the argument against Mill's theory in a more explicit form: Speakers of English judge that (64) is true while (63) is not; therefore, by (O) these two sentences are not synonymous. Since, however, (64) is the result of substituting 'Phosphorus' by 'Hesperus' in (63) it follows by (L) that these names are not synonymous either. But since the names are coreferential this conclusion contradicts (M).

Note that the argument is theory independent to a large degree. *Any* theory of language that accepts (M) as well as (L) will run into problems of the Hesperus-Phosphorus kind. *No* theory can be Millian, compositional *and* empirically adequate. This consideration greatly diminishes the search space for the root of trouble. If a theory conforms to (M), (L) and (O) we should not accuse any of its other features of being the source of paradox. More specifically, in a Montagovian context it is not the adoption of a possible world semantics that we should blame for our problems. It is also not the fact that Montague's theory is total rather than partial that should be held responsible. In the preceding chapters we have seen a partialization of the standard theory and it is clear that it still suffers from the antinomies, but this is only to be expected from a theory that conforms to (M) and (L). It is the conjunction of these two principles and these two principles alone that is to blame for the bad predictions that we have derived from them.

The combination of principles (L) and (O) provides us with a method for distinguishing meanings. We can question any alleged synonymy between two expressions by putting the two into the larger context of a sentence. If this results in a possible difference in truth value, then the two expressions were not synonymous after all. This is essentially what we did in the Introduction. At first sight one might consider the sentences 'John walks' and 'John walks and Bill talks or does not talk' to be equivalent in meaning, since after all by ordinary propositional logic they entail each other. However, by putting them into the context 'Mary believes that___' we have seen that they are not synonymous; the two resulting sentences may differ in truth value. As a consequence we found that a more fine-grained relation of synonymy was needed and we proceeded to produce one.

This method of distinguishing meanings is an instance of a *method of contrast* that is generally used in linguistics. Compare the way in which categories are obtained in syntax: two expressions belong to the same category if interchanging one for the other in the context of any sentence does not affect well-formedness judgements of speakers. A similar method is used in phonology to obtain equivalence classes of sounds (a phoneme is the union of certain of these classes). Our version of the Fregean argument against (M) is an application of the method of contrast in semantics and we shall shortly see another example of such an application when we discuss some modern responses to Russell's theory that an ordinary proper name like 'Romulus' is just short for a description like 'the man who killed Remus and founded Rome'.

The method of contrast is a very powerful tool in discriminating between meanings and in fact we might worry if it does not lead to an account of synonymy between expressions that is *too* fine-grained. Mates 1952 notes a curious consequence of the assumption that synonymy is subjected to Leibniz's Law.[2] Using the method of contrast, it is possible to show that pairs of terms that count as paradigms of synonymy, pairs like 'bachelor' and 'unmarried man', or 'doctor' and 'physician', are not synonymous after all, since they do not conform to the strict standard set by the principle. Consider the following pair.

(65) Whoever believes that Bill is a doctor believes that Bill is a doctor

(66) Whoever believes that Bill is a doctor believes that Bill is a physician

---

[2]Mates' formulation of the interchangeability principle is thus:

Two expressions are synonymous in a language L if and only if they may be interchanged in each sentence in L without altering the truth value of that sentence.

Note how close Mates' formulation is to Leibniz's:

Eadem sunt quorum unum potest substitui alteri salva veritate.

Clearly, (65) is true in all circumstances, but according to ordinary untutored judgement (66) need not be; in fact it is quite possible that (67) is true while (68) is not.

(67) Marie believes that Bill is a doctor

(68) Marie believes that Bill is a physician

Marie may believe that Bill is a doctor while not believing that he is a physician if she is confused about the correct criteria under which the predicate 'physician' applies. She may think for instance that physicians are a certain kind of physicists (assume Marie is Dutch) and she may believe that Bill is a doctor but that he is no such physicist. To my intuition (67) and the negation of (68) may correctly be used to report Marie's wrongheaded beliefs on such an occasion. By the method of contrast it follows that 'doctor' is not synonymous with 'physician'.

Not everybody shares my judgement that (67) and (68) might differ in truth value.[3] But, as Mates points out, denying that they might will not help to evade the seemingly strange conclusion that 'doctor' and 'physician' do not mean the same. For it can hardly be denied that in some possible circumstances (69) is true while (70) is false.

(69) Nobody doubts that (65)

(70) Nobody doubts that (66)

For example, as I have just stated, *I* doubt that whoever believes that Bill is a doctor believes that Bill is a physician. You may disagree but it seems impossible to deny me my doubt; and the conclusion that the meanings of 'doctor' and 'physician' must be distinguished can be drawn on the basis of the non-synonymy of sentences (69) and (70).

The conclusion is perhaps surprising but it is not problematic. In the previous chapter we have seen how to obtain a relatively weak, coarse-grained relation of synonymy from a strong, fine-grained one with the help of a set of locally active meaning postulates. We may use the weak relation as an explication of the notion of synonymity as it is ordinarily used, but it is the strong notion that we are after presently. Note that adding

MP4 $\lambda i \forall x \, (doctor \, xi = physician \, xi)$

as a meaning postulate to the theory given in the previous chapters will ensure that doctor will be weakly synonymous (but not strongly synonymous) to physician and that Bill is a doctor will be weakly synonymous to Bill is a physician. But Marie believes that Bill is a doctor will not be weakly synonymous to Marie believes that Bill is a physician in that case. The relevant meaning postulate must hold locally but it may fail to hold in some

<hr>

[3]Putnam 1954 says that he does not doubt that whoever believes that all Greeks are Greeks believes that all Greeks are Hellenes (but adds that he thinks that somebody else may doubt it).

of Marie's doxastic alternatives. That every doctor is a physician holds by linguistic convention, but Marie, who is not in full command of the English language, fails to know it.

We see here that however fine-grained a notion of synonymy the method of contrast forces us to adopt, by adopting local postulates we can always get a coarser grain on those expressions that do not involve intensional contexts. Even if we would strengthen the relation of synonymy to the point were it is coextensive or almost coextensive with the relation of syntactic identity of expressions we can get an ordinary entailment relation outside of intensional contexts.

Let us return to the question of Millianism and let us follow Geach in calling a context *Shakespearean* if coreferential names can be interchanged in it *salva veritate* (a rose / By any other name, would smell as sweet). Then on a purely Millian account it would follow that all contexts in ordinary English are Shakespearean (provided (L) is accepted). In other words, on this account the following principle of *Substitutivity* must be accepted.

(S) *Coreferential names are interchangeable salva veritate.*

We may however distinguish weaker forms of Millianism, for it is of course possible to hold that some contexts are Shakespearean while others are not. At first glance it may seem for example that in *Naming and Necessity* (Kripke 1972), the famous paper that reintroduced Millianism into the philosophy of language, such a weaker form is defended. For although it is argued in this article that *modal* contexts are Shakespearean and that sentences (71) and (72) below are both true, it seems that contexts of *epistemic* necessity should be counted as nonShakespearean, since the author accepts the truth of (73),[4] while he does not accept (74).

(71) Necessarily Hesperus is Hesperus

(72) Necessarily Hesperus is Phosphorus

(73) We do not know a priori that Hesperus is Phosphorus

(74) We do not know a priori that Hesperus is Hesperus

The pure form of Mill's theory is in conflict with the position taken in *Naming and Necessity* that true identity statements are necessary but not known a priori.

In a later paper (Kripke 1979) however, Kripke moves towards a more radical form of the Millian doctrine and gives an interesting argument that is meant to cast doubt on—what he calls—the 'received platitude' that (S) should be rejected. The argument shows that the Millian theory of names is not a necessary ingredient in the derivation of paradoxes of the Hesperus-Phosphorus kind and it does this by giving two principles that suffice to

---

[4]This sentence can be found on the last page of the second lecture of the work mentioned.

derive paradoxical conclusions of the same sort without any assumption of Millianism. The first of these is a *disquotational principle*.

(D) If a normal English speaker, on reflection, sincerely assents to '*p*', then he believes that *p*.

The second principle is the principle of translation.

(Tr) If a sentence of one language expresses a truth in that language, then any translation of it into any other language also expresses a truth (in that other language).

Now consider Pierre who is a native of Paris and a speaker of French but who has, at some stage in his life, moved to London and learned English there. By coincidence Pierre has never learned that the city he now lives in, the city he refers to as 'London' in English, is the city that he calls 'Londres' in his native language.

Back in Paris Pierre has heard some things from the British Tourist Office that made him sincerely assent to the French sentence 'Londres est jolie', but now, living in a depressing area of the city, he assents to the English sentence 'London is not pretty'. Not having found any reason to revise his opinions about 'Londres', however, he still assents to 'Londres est jolie'.

Now by an application of (D) we find that

(75) Pierre believes that London is not pretty

is true. On the other hand, the French version of this principle allows us to infer the truth of:

(76) Pierre croit que Londres est jolie.

But this is conventionally translated as

(77) Pierre believes that London is pretty,

and it follows by (Tr) that we must ascribe inconsistent beliefs to Pierre. This is paradoxical for there need not be anything wrong with Pierre's reasoning capacities; Pierre may be a perfect logician for all that we know, it is unfair to accuse him of any logical density. We have derived a paradoxical result from the premises (D) and (Tr).

Now, Kripke argues, the usual refutation of Substitutivity is based on an acceptance of principle (D). We reject (S) because Quine's Jones can sincerely say 'Cicero denounced Cataline. Tully didn't' and from this, by (D), (78) and (79) follow.

(78) Jones believes that Cicero denounced Cataline

(79) Jones believes that Tully didn't denounce Cataline

But if (S) were to hold we could derive (80) from (79)

(80) Jones believes that Cicero didn't denounce Cataline.

And it is no less unreasonable to accuse Jones of inconsistent beliefs than it is unreasonable to ascribe a lack of logical acumen to Pierre.

Principles (S) and (D) are not compatible, but (still according to Kripke) it would be a mistake to put the blame for the antinomies on (S) one-sidedly since—as we have seen from Pierre's puzzle—paradoxical results can already be obtained if (S) is replaced by the innocent translation principle (Tr). Kripke even suggests that (D) *alone* is enough to obtain paradoxical results:

> The usual use of Jones's case as a counterexample to the substitutivity principle is [...], I think, somewhat analogous to the following sort of procedure. Someone wishes to give a *reductio ad absurdum* argument against a hypothesis in topology. He does succeed in refuting this hypothesis, but his derivation of an absurdity from the hypothesis makes essential use of the unrestricted comprehension schema in set theory, which he regards as self-evident. (In particular, the class of all classes not members of themselves plays a key role in his argument.) Once we know that the unrestricted comprehension schema and the Russell class lead to contradiction by themselves, it is clear that it was an error to blame the earlier contradiction on the topological hypothesis.
>
> The situation would have been the same if, after deducing a contradiction from the topological hypothesis plus the 'obvious' unrestricted comprehension schema, it was found that a similar contradiction followed if we replaced the topological hypothesis by an apparently 'obvious' premise. In both cases it would be clear that, even though we may still not be confident of any specific flaw in the argument against the topological hypothesis, blaming the contradiction on that hypothesis is illegitimate: rather we are in a 'paradoxical' area where it is unclear *what* has gone wrong.
>
> It is my suggestion, then, that the situation with respect to the interchangeability of codesignative names is similar. True, such a principle, when combined with our normal disquotational judgements of belief, leads to straightforward absurdities. But [...] the 'same' absurdities can be derived by replacing the interchangeability principle by our normal practices of translation and disquotation, or even by disquotation alone.

Are we committed to a defense of (D), the principle that is compared to unrestricted comprehension here? Strictly speaking we are not, for our rejection of Mill's theory was not based on that principle but on the principle of observational adequacy (O); (D) is not used *essentially* in the Fregean *reductio*. The differences between (D) and (O) are important. While (D) pertains only to belief sentences, principle (O) pertains to all sentences whatsoever and while (D) could be rejected without causing any damage to the rest of the theory, it seems that (O) is essential to empirical semantics. Moreover, any suggestion that the conjunction of (L) and (O) be inconsistent can easily be countered by the following trivial consistency proof: Suppose that we have a derivation of a contradiction from the premises (L) and (O); then in this derivation change the words 'is synonymous with' by 'is syntactically identical with' throughout. The result will be a derivation of a contradiction from obviously true premises, which shows that some mistake must have been made.

But although we are not strictly committed to the principle of disquotation it must be admitted that our acceptance of (O) strongly suggests acceptance of (D), for it seems that the semantical judgements of language users conform to this last principle to a large degree. I think that there is hardly any reason to suspect (D) of inconsistency. There is a far more obvious candidate for this suspicion.

Let us see how Kripke attempts to show that (D) *alone* leads to absurdity. To this end Peter is considered, a man who has heard about the Polish musician Paderewski. Peter asserts: 'Paderewski is a fine musician' and so from (D) we may conclude:

(81) Peter believes that Paderewski is a fine musician.

Peter has also heard about a certain Paderewski who is a Polish politician. In fact the politician and the musician are one and the same person, but Peter does not connect them, and since he does not think highly about the musical capacities of Middle European statesmen he asserts: 'Paderewski is a bad musician'. From this we may infer:

(82) Peter believes that Paderewski is a bad musician.

Again we have a paradoxical result. It seems that we must ascribe inconsistent beliefs to Peter while intuitively there is no reason for doing so. This time it seems we have only used principle (D) to arrive at the awkward conclusion.

If this argument were really correct (D)'s future would look dim, but (as Kripke admits in a footnote) in fact we need (Tr) as well as (D) here to get the bad result. The illusion that only (D) is involved rests on a subtle fallacy. Surely there is a slight difference between Peter's English and ours. In Peter's English there are *two* names 'Paderewski', used homonymously, where in our language there is only *one* such name. This means that, although we can apply a disquotational principle to Peter's words, the results of applying this principle will not be sentences in our language; they will be framed in Peter's ideolect. Application of the principle must be restricted to those cases where the sentence inside quotes strictly belongs to the same language as the language that the principle itself is framed in. The slightest violation of this restriction may result in anomaly.

A similar restriction holds for that other famous principle of disquotation: Tarski's Convention (T).

(T) 'p' is true if and only if p.

Here too the p inside quotes can only be instantiated by a sentence of the language that the principle itself is formulated in and even a minimal deviation from this rule may wreak havoc. Imagine someone who mixes up the two modal logicians C.I. Lewis and D. Lewis. Such a person would use *one* name 'Lewis' where we use *two* names, 'Lewis$_1$' and 'Lewis$_2$', say. Suppose we point him out his mistake and tell him that Lewis$_1$ isn't Lewis$_2$. Then he could 'prove', reasoning *in* his language but *about* ours, that 'Lewis$_1$ is Lewis$_2$' is true if we would allow him that

(83) 'Lewis$_1$ is Lewis$_2$' is true if and only if Lewis is Lewis.

But we cannot allow him this and (83) is not a correct instantiation of Tarski's Convention.

If instantiations of (D) are restricted in a way that is similar to the way instantiations of (T) are restricted, we can use the disquotational principle only to derive sentences (81) and (82) *conceived of as sentences in Peter's language*, but as such their conjunction does not ascribe an inconsistency to Peter, no more than 'Muskens believes that Lewis$_2$ wrote *Counterfactuals* but that Lewis$_1$ didn't' ascribes an inconsistency to me. To obtain a paradox from (81) and (82) we must use (Tr) to translate these sentences homophonically from Peter's language into ours.

So it seems that the use of premise (Tr) cannot be eliminated from Kripke's arguments. I know of no other argument that shows that (D) in itself leads to anomalies. From this we cannot of course conclude that (D) is safe, but now our suspicion is raised: if it is so hard to get rid of (Tr) as a premise from the derivation of the antinomies, is then this principle as innocent as it is supposed to be?

It is not. In fact Kripke himself shows that from (Tr) we can derive instances of (S).

In Hebrew there are two names for Germany, transliterable roughly as '*Ashkenaz*' and '*Germaniah*'—the first of these may be somewhat archaic. When Hebrew sentences are translated into English, both become 'Germany'. [...] there is [...] an argument for substitutivity, based on the principle of translation. Translate a Hebrew sentence involving '*Ashkenaz*' into English, so that '*Ashkenaz*' goes into '*Germany*'. Then retranslate the result into Hebrew, this time translating 'Germany' as '*Germaniah*'. By the principle of translation, both translations preserve truth value. So: the truth value of any sentence of Hebrew involving '*Ashkenaz*' remains the same when '*Ashkenaz*' is replaced by '*Germaniah*'—a 'proof' of substitutivity! A similar 'proof' can be provided wherever there are two names in one language, and a normal practice of translating both indifferently into a single name of another language.

In Dutch there are two different names for the town that is called 'The Hague' in English; the first of these is 'Den Haag', the second is ''s-Gravenhage'. Both names are perfectly acceptable in standard Dutch; both are conventionally translated as 'The Hague' and this name in its turn can either be translated as 'Den Haag' or as ''s-Gravenhage'. The situation matches the 'Ashkenaz'-'Germaniah' case exactly. The Dutch sentence

(84) Piet vindt dat Den Haag saai is

is conventionally translated into

(85) Piet thinks that The Hague is dull

and this sentence can be retranslated as

(86) Piet vindt dat 's-Gravenhage saai is.

Conversely, (85) is a standard translation of (86) while (84) conventionally translates (85). Applying (Tr) twice leads to the conclusion that (84) and (86) must have the same truth value. But Dutch language users characteristically judge that these sentences might differ in truth value, just as English speakers judge that (63) and (64) do. Hence the translation principle leads to a variant of the classical puzzle (note that we have *only* used the translation principle here). The principle is at odds with our principle of observational adequacy and it should therefore be rejected. Translation does not always preserve truth.

This conclusion may be surprising (although it confirms an old wisdom: *traduttore traditore*). But if it is, our surprise may be mitigated somewhat by the consideration that our findings in no way contradict that in *some* cases—in all cases not involving intensional contexts—translation preserves truth automatically and that in other cases truth is preserved conditionally. For example, if the French sentence 'Pierre croit que Londres est jolie' is true, then 'Pierre believes that London is pretty' is true *provided* that Pierre makes the conventional connections. Translating the French sentence into the English one amounts to the assertion that Pierre knows that 'London' and 'Londres' (and 'pretty' and 'joli') are codesignative. In some cases, in particular in the case we have at hand, this is just false and in these circumstances the translation is incorrect.

I conclude that Kripke's attempt at a refutation of the Fregean argument against (M) fails. Firstly, the refutation assumes that Frege's argument must be based on the disquotational principle, a principle Kripke suspects to be paradoxical. But we do not need this premise, since we can replace it by the consistent principle (O). Secondly, the refutation does not work even if we allow Frege's argument to be based on (D) rather than on (O). Let us accept (D) for the moment. Why, on the Fregean account, is (S) and hence (M) to be rejected? Because (D) + (S) lead to anomaly. Jones's case can be taken as an example, as we have done above, but we can also use the case of Piet, the Dutch language user who earnestly says: 'Den Haag is saai. 's-Gravenhage niet.' From this by (D) not only (84) follows but (87) follows as well.

(87) Piet vindt dat 's-Gravenhage niet saai is

On the other hand (86) follows from (84) by principle (S) and the conjunction of (86) and (87) is anomalous since it ascribes an inconsistency to Piet.

We have of course used only one instance of (S) here: the statement that (86) is true if (84) is. Call this statement (S_0); as was seen above (Tr) entails (S_0). Kripke's attempt at a refutation of the Fregean argument is based on the observation (from Pierre's case) that (D) + (Tr) lead to paradox. But this is completely unsurprising since (D) + (S_0) already do. Can a *reductio* argument be countered by strengthening the premise which was to be refuted?

A defense of the view that names are descriptions

If the meaning of a name is not the thing named, then what do names mean? We must now try to answer this question and it is natural to turn to Russell's Theory of Descriptions at this point. On Russell's account ordinary names (in contradistinction to what he calls 'logically proper names') are definite descriptions in disguise and 'Socrates', for example, is just short for a description like 'the philosopher who drank the hemlock'. This theory has met with serious objections (I shall address some of them below), but even if the theory is problematic in some of its aspects, up till now it seems to be the only theory capable of strict formalization that deals with the Hesperus-Phosphorus problem adequately. Roughly: if 'Hesperus' abbreviates 'the planet seen at dusk' and if 'Phosphorus' is short for 'the planet seen at dawn', then 'Hesperus is Phosphorus' is analyzed as 'The planet seen at dusk is the planet seen at dawn', an epistemically contingent sentence. 'Hesperus is Hesperus', on the other hand, means 'The planet seen at dusk is the planet seen at dusk' on this account, and is epistemically necessary.

Russell's theory does not only solve the Hesperus-Phosphorus problem, it also gives an account of the *scope sensitivity* of proper names. For example, one reading of the sentence 'Zeus isn't bald' implies Zeus's existence, the other does not. Since in Russell's theory the name 'Zeus' is shorthand for (say) 'the King of the Olympian gods', the ambiguity is readily explained: one reading of the sentence is 'There is exactly one King of the Olympian gods and he isn't bald', the other is 'It is not true that there is exactly one King of the Olympian gods and that he is bald'. The first of these readings entails the existence of the King of the Olympian gods, the other does not.

We see that the scope of a name can interact with the scope of a negation here, but it can also interact with the scope of an intensional context. Suppose Mary is at a party of the local Philosophy Department. The party is a masked ball and Mary is presently talking to a man who is dressed up as the Hooded Man. She does not recognize the man but from certain clues in his conversation she forms the opinion that this is her colleague Bill. In fact she is wrong, it is John who she is talking to. In this case in a sense it is true that

(88) Mary thinks that John is Bill.

In another sense this is false. Mary thinks *of* John: he is Bill. Of course she does not think: John is Bill. Again it is unproblematic to account for this difference in the Russellian theory, but on a standard account of names the two readings will collapse.

In as far as Russell's description theory of names was designed to solve problems of the kind illustrated here, logical puzzles that arise in connection with names, it can be called a *logical* theory of naming or a theory of the *meaning* of names. But there is a second description theory of names that was generally confused with the first one until Kripke 1972 separated the two. This theory is what Kripke calls the description theory of *reference*; it is not a theory about the logical properties of names in ordinary language, but it is a theory that intends to solve the riddle *how names refer*, how reference comes about.

What, then, is the description theory of reference? Kripke 1972 describes it very accurately, but for the present purpose a simplified version of his account will do: the description theory of the reference of names is the theory that each speaker A associates with each proper name X of the language a property φ such that the following hold:

(a) A believes that X is a φ
(b) A believes φ to single out some individual uniquely
(c) If there really is some unique individual satisfying φ then that individual is the referent of X,
(d) otherwise X does not refer.

For example, a person may link the property 'pupil of Socrates and master of Aristotle' to the name 'Plato', believing that Plato taught Aristotle and was taught by Socrates and that nobody else had both these properties. Then this person refers to Plato using the name 'Plato' if and only if his belief is in fact correct and Plato is the unique person who was a pupil of Socrates and a teacher of Aristotle.

This picture of the way in which names refer seems compelling enough, but Kripke gives some very simple and very convincing counterexamples. Consider someone who knows very little about Roman history, so that, when asked: 'Who was Cicero?', he can only come up with the answer that Cicero was a famous Roman orator. The example seems realistic enough. The predicate 'famous Roman orator' does of course not single out anybody in particular, but even so, our person can use the name 'Cicero' to refer to Cicero, saying things like 'Cicero must have been happy'. So here we have a counterexample against (d): 'Cicero' refers even while 'famous Roman orator' does not identify uniquely. The same example will refute (b) if we assume that our speaker does not *believe* that 'famous Roman orator' singles out one particular person.

There are also counterexamples against (c). Probably many people heard the name 'Peano' for the first time when they heard about the Peano axioms (I certainly did). It is of course natural in this situation to conjecture that Peano was the discoverer of the Peano axioms. But this is false: in fact the axioms were discovered by Dedekind. Now according to the description theory of reference many people refer to Dedekind when they use the name Peano, since it is he who uniquely fulfills the description ('the discoverer of the Peano axioms') they associate with this name. For instance, when such a person asks: 'Was Peano an Italian?', he is really asking whether Dedekind was an Italian. This is nonsense of course.

There are variants of the description theory of reference that are more complex and more sophisticated than the simple one I have outlined above. Searle's proposal that sets of properties rather than single ones be associated with names is one of them. But it seems that for each variant of the theory counterexamples can be given that are variants of those given by Kripke. I will not discuss any of these complications here (I refer the reader to Kripke and to the vast literature on the subject), but it is pretty clear that complicating the theory will not save it.

So the description theory of reference must fall; but we needn't shed a tear for it, for it is a theory that is quite alien to our purposes. We are after a characterization of the logic of natural language and there is no reason to assume that a characterization of this kind presupposes a theory of the reference of names of the kind sketched above. Besides, even if such a theory could be found, what would be gained by it? Even if each name could be associated with a predicate such that (a)–(d) above would hold, we would only have reduced the question how *names* refer to the question how their defining *predicates* refer. I see no sense in this.

Let us therefore return to the *logical* version of the Description Theory of naming, the theory that the *meaning* of a name is a description. There is an objection against this theory too. It can be found in Searle 1958.

Suppose we agree to drop "Aristotle" and use, say, "the teacher of

Alexander", then it is a necessary truth that the man referred to is Alexander's teacher—but it is a contingent fact that Aristotle ever went into pedagogy...

Note that this argument is really an application of the method of contrast discussed above. If 'Aristotle' would be synonymous with 'the teacher of Alexander', then, by substitution, the following two sentences should be synonymous as well.

(89) Necessarily Aristotle is Aristotle

(90) Necessarily Aristotle is the teacher of Alexander

But they aren't and so the assumption is false.

This shows—by an argument that is completely analogous to the argument that refutes (M)—that the Description Theory of names as it was formulated by Russell is not adequate for our purposes. But the theory can be simplified to a form that is adequate.

Quine 1953, after having described the description theory of names, continues:

> In order (...) to subsume a one-word name or alleged name such as 'Pegasus' under Russell's theory of description, we must, of course, be able first to translate the word into a description. But this is no real restriction. If the notion of Pegasus had been so obscure or so basic a one that no pat translation into a descriptive phrase had offered itself along familiar lines, we could still have availed ourselves of the following artificial and trivial-seeming device: we could have appealed to the *ex hypothesi* unanalyzable, irreducible attribute of *being Pegasus*, adopting, for its expression, the verb 'is-Pegasus', or 'pegasizes'. The noun 'Pegasus' itself could then be treated as derivative, and identified after all with a description: 'the thing that is-Pegasus', 'the thing that pegasizes'.

Quine's proposal weakens the original Description Theory. In order to see this, we may conversely think of Russell's theory as strengthening Quine's. The theory that 'Pegasus' should be analyzed as, say, 'the winged horse that was captured by Bellopheron' (Quine's example) can be assumed to consist of two parts: (a) that the name is to be identified with the description 'the pegasizer', and (b) that 'pegasizer' is to be identified with the predicate 'winged horse that was captured by Bellopheron'. The conjunction of these two is equivalent to Russell's proposal; Quine accepts (a) but rejects (b). I find this highly interesting, for it is (a) that may boast of the successes of the Description Theory, but it is (b) that is responsible for its failures. The reason why Russell's theory of ordinary proper names works so extremely well is that it gives names the *form* of descriptions, not because it equates their meanings with the meanings of particular descriptions in language.

It does this last thing too and this causes the trouble we have met with, but the fact that it does seems to be a minor feature of the theory, a bug that is easily removed. We can remove it by dropping (b). Doing this does not impair the explanatory power of the theory, the theory's 'capacity for dealing with puzzles' in Russell's phrase, but it does block the derivation of odd consequences like the equivalence of (89) and (90).

Let us formalize Quine's idea and give a new translation to the proper names occurring in our fragment of English. We shall no longer translate them as individual constants that are 'lifted' to the level of quantifiers, but shall stipulate that names translate as terms that have the form of definite descriptions instead. In the translation of a name like Aristotle the role of the 'Aristotalizer' predicate will be played by a constant of type $\langle es \rangle$, Aristotle.

$$\text{Aristotle}^\circ = \lambda P \lambda i \exists x \, (\forall y (Aristotle \, yi \leftrightarrow x = y) \wedge Pxi)$$

Proper names other than Aristotle are translated in a similar way.

Since names are now translated as descriptions the present proposal certainly should count as a description theory of names. But let us beware of drawing the wrong conclusion that the proposal hence is incompatible with the Millian view. This is not so. In fact, it is easy to see that the new translation induces a weaker logic (a stronger relation of entailment) on our fragment of English than the original translation did: to recover the original, Millian, account of naming one need only augment the present theory with an axiom that makes names into *rigid designators*.

(R) $\exists x \, (\delta = \lambda y \lambda i \, (x = y))$,

where δ is $Aristotle_{\langle es \rangle}$, $John_{\langle es \rangle}$, $Bill_{\langle es \rangle}$, $Mary_{\langle es \rangle}$ etc.

This axiom stipulates that there is some possible individual such that the 'Aristotalizer' predicate uniquely picks out that individual in every situation. Clearly, the old way of translating names and the new one lead to the same relation of entailment and hence to the same problems if the latter would be combined with the adoption of (R). I shall therefore not adopt it. But below I shall close the gap between the present position and the now standard theory of names halfway by accepting some of (R)'s consequences.

First, however, let us compare the present position with the *full* Description Theory, the theory that is attacked in *Naming and Necessity*. Our theory is weaker than this theory too: if an orthodox Description Theorist should want 'Aristotle' to mean 'the teacher of Alexander' he could accept our account thus far, but would have to insist on adding an axiom that equates the 'Aristotalizer' predicate with the predicate 'teacher of Alexander'.

(91) $Aristotle = \lambda x \lambda j \exists y \, (\forall z (Alexander \, zj \leftrightarrow z = y) \wedge teach \, xyj)$

Allowing (91) to be accepted would ruin our weak description theory. It would lead to the incorrect prediction that (89) and (90) are equivalent, just as accepting (R) would lead to the wrong result that (63) and (64) are. So again we shall not adopt the axiom. But the fact that we can augment our theory in order to obtain the full Description Theory of meaning, just as we can strengthen it to get a version of the rigid designator theory, shows that our theory is weaker than both these classical accounts of naming. Ours is a *minimal* theory of names; it predicts that an entailment in natural language is valid only if both Russell's and Kripke's theories predict it to be valid.

This observation brings us in a rather comfortable position as far as the positive part of the theory is concerned, for it shows that any real counterexample to this part must have the very interesting property that it refutes *both* classical theories as well. Of course it is very well possible to argue that the present account is too weak, that it predicts too few valid arguments, but an adherent to either of the classical theories cannot argue that it predicts too many, on pain of contradicting himself.

(R) can be written as the conjunction of the following two sentences.

(92) $\forall i \exists x \forall y \, (\delta y i = (x = y))$ (Total Function)

(93) $\forall i j \forall x \, (\delta x i = \delta x j)$ (Absolute Rigidity)
   where δ is *Aristotle, John* etc.

The first of these says that the converses of the Aristotalizer predicate and its likes are total functions (so in Montagovian terms these are individual concepts, functions from possible situations to possible things). The second makes them into constant functions (so Absolute Rigidity is closely analogous to Montague's first meaning postulate in PTQ). The latter requirement we cannot accept, but we may well accept a slightly weakened version of the first. Let us stipulate that the predicates are partial functions.

AX16 $\forall i \exists x \forall y \, (\delta y i \rightarrow (x = y))$ (Partial Function)
   where δ is *Aristotle, John* etc.

Note that this axiom does not strengthen the logic of our fragment, since in no translation the predicates *Aristotle, John* etc. can occur outside the context of a description. But the axiom simplifies things somewhat, since it is now possible to write Aristotle° as the term $\lambda P \lambda i \exists x \, (Aristotle \; xi \wedge Pxi)$ and translations of other names can be written in a similar way.

Let us see in some detail how the Description Theory of names, incorporated now into our Montagovian framework, solves the puzzles of naming that Russell intended it to solve. In (95) and (96) we find the straightforward readings of Jones knows that Tully talks and of Jones knows that Cicero talks respectively, and clearly the conjunction of the first with (94), Tully is Cicero, does not entail the second.

(94) Tully is Cicero
$[\text{Tully}[\text{be Cicero}]^5]^4$
$\lambda i \exists x \, (\text{Tully } xi \wedge \text{Cicero } xi)$

(95) Jones knows that Tully talks
$[\text{Jones}[\text{know that}[\text{Tully talk}]^4]^7]^4$
$\lambda i \exists x \, (\text{Jones } xi \wedge \forall j \, (K x j i \rightarrow T \exists y \, (\text{Tully } yj \wedge \text{talk } yj)))$

(96) Jones knows that Cicero talks
$[\text{Jones}[\text{know that}[\text{Cicero talk}]^4]^7]^4$
$\lambda i \exists x \, (\text{Jones } xi \wedge \forall j \, (K x j i \rightarrow T \exists y \, (\text{Cicero } yj \wedge \text{talk } yj)))$

Although Tully may talk at all of Jones's epistemic alternatives, he may fail to be Cicero at some of them.

This deals with the main point, the fact that coreferential names cannot freely be intersubstituted in propositional attitude contexts, but there are minor points as well. The following example shows that the theory allows for non-trivial scope distinctions resulting from the interplay between names and intensional contexts. The first reading of the sentence shown says that Mary believes *about* John that he is Bill; the second says that she believes: John is Bill.

(97) Mary believes that John is Bill
$[\text{John}[\text{Mary}[\text{believe that}[\text{he}_0[\text{be Bill}]^5]^4]^7]^4]^{14,0}$
$\lambda i \exists xy \, (\text{John } xi \wedge \text{Mary } yi \wedge \forall j \, (B y j i \rightarrow T \text{Bill } xj)$

(98) Mary believes that John is Bill
$[\text{Mary}[\text{believe that}[\text{John }[\text{be Bill}]^5]^4]^7]^4$
$\lambda i \exists y \, (\text{Mary } yi \wedge \forall j \, (B y j i \rightarrow T \exists x \, (\text{John } xj \wedge \text{Bill } xj))$

The interplay between names and negations gives scope distinctions too, as we see from the two different readings of Zeus does not walk below.

(99) Zeus does not walk
$[\text{Zeus walk}]^{17}$
$\lambda i \neg \exists x \, (\text{Zeus } xi \wedge \text{walk } xi)$

(100) Zeus does not walk
$[\text{Zeus}[\text{he}_0 \text{ walk}]^{17}]^{14,0}$
$\lambda i \exists x \, (\text{Zeus } xi \wedge \neg \text{walk } xi)$

Clearly, the scope distinction between (99) and (100) would collapse if we would translate Zeus as $\lambda P \, (P \text{ zeus})$ in the old way, or even if we would just adopt *Total Function*. The distinction between (97) and (98) would vanish on the adoption of *Total Function* and *Absolute Rigidity*, and the latter principle alone is enough to make (94) and (95) entail (96).

But not all evidence pleads against *Absolute Rigidity*, since not all intensional contexts in English behave in a similar way. Although coreferential names cannot always be interchanged *salva veritate* in epistemic and doxastic contexts there is an intuition that they can be so interchanged in modal ones. According to this view modal contexts are Shakespearean. So for example, in Kripke 1972 it is argued that (101) entails (102).

(101) Hesperus is Phosphorus

(102) Necessarily Hesperus is Phosphorus

Is this correct? Is it necessary that Hesperus is Phosphorus? Much seems to depend on the *kind* of necessity that is involved here. In particular it seems important whether it is *logical* necessity or *metaphysical* necessity that is at stake. If the first of these is meant, I protest: in no existing account of logic will the truth of an identity statement $a = b$ in one model entail its truth in all of them; so I don't see why an identity statement should be true in all situations if it is true in one. On the other hand, I admit that there is a restricted sense of necessity in which (102) is true. It is in this sense, the sense that I shall call 'metaphysical' for lack of a better word, that Hesperus might not have been anything but Phosphorus. There is a sense of the word 'possible' in which models that do not assign the same object to the names 'Hesperus' and 'Phosphorus' do not count as possible situations; situations in which names that actually corefer do not have the same bearer are not metaphysically possible, even if they are logically possible.

We must distinguish then between logical necessity and metaphysical necessity, but for the sake of argument let us interpret the sentence adverb 'necessarily' in the second sense here and let us accept that (101) entails (102). We have a problem then, for while the standard theory predicts that *all* intensional contexts are Shakespearean, our description theory thus far predicts that *none* of them are. In fact it seems to be more correct to say that some are and some are not. This shows that we must strengthen our logic; but of course we should not make it collapse into the old theory.

Something else is wrong with the present treatment of the expressions necessarily and possibly as well. In order to state what it is, let me introduce in a very sketchy way the class of logics containing more than one intensional connective (see e.g. Goldblatt 1987 for some more detail). Syntactically these multimodal logics are just like ordinary propositional modal logic except that where the latter has only one intensional operator, $\Box$, the former have many, say $[i]$ for each element i of some index set I. The semantics too is obtained simply by generalizing that of ordinary modal logic: Define *frames* to be tuples $\langle W, \{R_i \mid i \in I\} \rangle$ comprising a set W with a collection of binary relations R_i over that set. Define *models* for this logic as tuples $\langle F, V \rangle$, where F is a frame and V is a valuation function assigning a subset of W to each propositional constant. With the help of the usual Tarski truth definition we can define the relation $M \models_w \varphi$, φ is true in M at world w. The crucial clause in this definition runs as follows:

$$M \models_w [i]\varphi \text{ iff for all } w' \in W, wR_iw' \text{ implies } M \models_{w'} \varphi.$$

A formula φ is *valid* if $M \models_w \varphi$ holds for all M and w.

This gives the weakest multimodal logic. Stronger logics can be obtained by imposing extra constraints on the accessibility relations R_i. For instance, if, for some i, we want $[i]$ to behave essentially like an *S5* operator, we may stipulate that R_i is an equivalence relation; if we want the schema $[i]\varphi \to [j]\varphi$ to be valid (for example when $[i]$ is to stand for 'John knows that___' and $[j]$ for 'John believes that___'), we should demand that $R_j \subseteq R_i$.

There is one possible constraint that has a special interest for us: we can let some special operator $[i]$ quantify over *all* elements of W by stipulating that the corresponding accessibility relation R_i is the universal relation $\{\langle w, w' \rangle \mid w, w' \in W\}$. Let's write $\square$ for this special $[i]$; we then have:

$$M \models_w \square\varphi \text{ iff } M \models_{w'} \varphi \text{ for all } w' \in W.$$

The operator $\square$ is now what is called an *outer* operator. The move has two consequences. The first is that, since the universal relation is an equivalence relation, $\square$ gets an *S5* logic, and the second is that since all R_j are now contained in R_i, the schema $\square\varphi \to [j]\varphi$ will be valid for all $j \in I$ (we even have that $\square\varphi \to [j_1]\ldots[j_n]\varphi$ will be valid for all $j_1, \ldots, j_n \in I$).

Thus far we have treated the expression necessarily as if it were a priviliged outer operator like $\square$ above, but are we willing to accept the consequences? That necessarily gets an *S5* logic I find perfectly acceptable (although other options are possible of course), but the second consequence I find hard to swallow. I do not think, for example, that (104) below follows from (103), or that (105) does.

(103) Necessarily every ophtalmologist is an oculist

(104) Every man knows that every ophtalmologist is an oculist

(105) Every woman believes that every man knows that every ophtalmologist is an oculist

Since 'Every ophtalmologist is an oculist' is analytically true, I take it that (103) is true as well. Situations in which some ophtalmologist is no oculist cannot arise, they should not count as possible situations in the strict sense. On the other hand, neither (104) nor (105) need be true. But this poses a problem, since on the present treatment of 'necessarily' the latter sentences follow from (103). In fact, the treatment causes a form of Mates's problem to reappear.

For a second example that shows that necessarily shouldn't be taken as the strongest of all intensional operators consider the following sentences.

(106) Necessarily Donald is a duck

(107) Everybody knows that Donald is a duck

There is a perfectly respectable philosophical position (a position that is strongly related to the view that names are rigid designators) that says that objects can have non-trivial essential properties. Membership of a natural kind is a property that is often quoted as such. Adherents of this view will hold e.g. that if some animal is a duck then it is a duck by necessity. So if Donald is a duck, then (106) is true. But this view would plainly become untenable if (107) would follow. Donald may be a duck without everybody knowing it. We see that if, as we assume here, 'everybody knows that___' acts as a universal intensional operator then either there are no essential properties (properties φ such that 'X is a φ' entails 'necessarily X is a φ') or 'necessarily' is not an outer operator.

It seems then that the expression 'necessarily' should not be given priviliged treatment. It belongs to the rank and file of intensional operators and should be treated as such. Its quantifying force should be restricted to a subset of the set of all situations, to those situations that are (*metaphysically*) *accessible from* a situation that is given. Technically it is easy to do this; let us write $\rho_{\langle ss \rangle}$ for the new accessibility relation and (re-)define:

$$\text{necessarily}^\circ \;=\; \lambda p \lambda i \forall j \, (\rho j i \rightarrow T p j)$$
$$\text{possibly}^\circ \;=\; \lambda p \lambda i \exists j \, (\rho j i \wedge T p j)$$

The translations of the modals are now in complete analogy with those of the doxastic and epistemic operators (except that the latter take subjects of course). In order to re-obtain $S5$ logic we can stipulate that the denotation and the complement of the antidenotation of ρ are equivalence relations.

AX17 $\forall i \, (\rho i i = \top)$

AX18 $\forall i j k \, ((\rho i j \wedge \rho j k) \twoheadrightarrow \rho i k))$

AX19 $\forall i j \, (\rho i j \twoheadrightarrow \rho j i)$

The relativization blocks the unwanted entailments: (109) below does not follow from (108) and (110) does not have (111) as a consequence.

(108) Necessarily every ophtalmologist is an oculist
[necessarily[[every ophtalmologist]^3 [be [a oculist]^3]^5]^4]^9
$\lambda i \forall j \, (\rho j i \rightarrow T \forall x \, (ophtalmologist \; xj \rightarrow oculist \; xj))$

(109) Every man knows that every ophtalmologist is an oculist
[[every man]^3 [know that [[every ophtalmologist]^3 [be
[a oculist]^3]^5]^4]^7]^4
$\lambda i \forall x \, (man \; xi \rightarrow T \forall j \, (K x j i \rightarrow \forall y \, (ophtalmologist \; yj \rightarrow oculist \; yj)))$

(110) Necessarily Donald is a duck
[necessarily [Donald [be [a duck]^3]^5]^4]^9
$\lambda i \forall j \, (\rho j i \rightarrow T \exists x \, (Donald \; xj \wedge duck \; xj))$

(111) Every man knows that Donald is a duck
[[every man]^3 [know that [Donald [be [a duck]^3]^5]^4]^7]^4
$\lambda i \forall x \, (man \; xi \rightarrow \forall j \, (K x j i \rightarrow T \exists y \, (Donald \; yj \wedge duck \; yj)))$

The derivations are blocked since there may be epistemically possible situations that are not metaphysically accessible.

We may go further. It seems that sentences like (108), sentences of the form necessarily S, where S is analytic, are not only true, but are analytically true themselves and should therefore be counted as weakly valid. Let us suppose that the analyticity of (108)'s embedded clause, 'Every ophtalmologist is an oculist', rests on the following meaning postulate.

MP5 $\lambda i \forall x \, (ophtalmologist \, xi = oculist \, xi)$

We can then capture the fact that (108) is analytic too by stipulating that meaning postulates must not only hold in the actual world, but at all accessible situations as well; no situation is accessible unless it conforms to our postulates.

MP6 $\lambda i \forall j \, (\rho j i \rightarrow \pi j)$, if π is a meaning postulate other than this one.

A first desirable consequence of this is that $\lambda i \forall j \, (\rho j i \rightarrow world \, j)$ is now a postulate: all accessible situations are total and coherent. As a result sentences like Necessarily every man talks or some man does not talk become weakly valid. This is as it should be. Another consequence is that, since the proposition

$$\lambda i \forall j \, (\rho j i \rightarrow \forall x \, (ophtalmologist \, xj = oculist \, xj))$$

is a postulate now, we are assured of the weak validity of (108).

In a similar way, if you are an essentialist, you may want to ensure the truth of (110) (or rather of 'Necessarily if Donald exists he's a duck') by stipulating that natural kind terms like the predicate 'being a duck' have the same extension in all accessible worlds:

(112) $\lambda i \forall j \, (\rho j i \rightarrow \forall x \, (duck \, xi = duck \, xj))$

Acceptance of (112) turns 'being a duck' into an internal property while it avoids obviously absurd consequences such as the derivability of (111) from 'Donald is a duck'.

We may call a predicate that has the same extension in all metaphysically accessible worlds *relatively rigid*. A predicate that has the same extension in *all* situations we may call *absolutely rigid*. A name is called absolutely (relatively) rigid if its underlying predicate is absolutely (relatively) rigid.

It is now clear how we can account for the fact that modals are Shakespearean, while avoiding the conclusion that belief contexts are. For although, as we have seen, the assumption that names are absolutely rigid leads to anomaly, we may well assume relative rigidity for names.

AX20 $\forall ij \, (\rho j i \rightarrow \forall x \, (\delta x i = \delta x j))$ (Relative Rigidity)
       where δ is *Aristotle, John* etc.

Under this assumption modals behave in the desired way, as we can see from the example below: (102) now follows from (101). But the move has no effect on the status of epistemic and doxastic contexts; the derivation of, say, (96) from (94) and (95) remains invalid.

(101) Hesperus is Phosphorus

[Hesperus[be Phosphorus]^5]^4

$\lambda i \exists x \, (Hesperus \, xi \wedge Phosphorus \, xi)$

(102) Necessarily Hesperus is Phosphorus

[necessarily [Hesperus[be Phosphorus]^5]^4]^4

$\lambda i \exists j \, (\rho j i \rightarrow T \exists x \, (Hesperus \, xj \wedge Phosphorus \, xj))$

The solution is simple, trivial even perhaps, but it works. On the one hand the paradoxes associated with names do no longer arise since names are now treated as logical descriptions. The description theory allows us to maintain that not all intensional contexts in English are Shakespearean. But on the other hand we are not driven to an opposite conclusion: some contexts in English may be Shakespearean while others are not. If empirical evidence suggests that some specific context is, we can formalize this by restricting the quantificational force of its translation to a (partial) set of situations on which names are rigid.

Treating modals in this way captures many of the intuitions that are usually taken to support the Millian position. What is the basic intuition behind the view on names that is advocated in *Naming and Necessity*? Kripke describes it thus:

> Although the idea is now a familiar one, I will give a brief restatement of the idea of rigid designation, and the intuition about names that underlies it. Consider:
>
> (a) Aristotle was fond of dogs
>
> A proper understanding of this statement involves an understanding both of the (extensionally correct) conditions under which it is in fact true, *and* of the conditions under which a counterfactual course of history, resembling the actual course in some respects but not in others, would be correctly (partially) described by (a). Presumably everyone agrees that there is a certain man—the philosopher we call 'Aristotle'— such that, as a matter of fact, (a) is true if and only if *he* was fond of dogs. The thesis of rigid designation is simply—subtle points aside— that the same paradigm applies to the truth conditions of (a) as it describes *counterfactual* situations. That is, (a) truly describes a counterfactual situation if and only if the same aforementioned man would have been fond of dogs, had that situation obtained.

But *this* we can very well accept, provided that the words 'counterfactual situation' are interpreted in a restricted sense. That is, while we cannot accept the view that (a) is true in any old situation if and only if the actual referent of the name 'Aristotle' was fond of dogs in that situation, we do hold that (a) truly describes a situation that may actually have arisen, a metaphysically accessible situation, if and only if the actual referent of 'Aristotle' would have been fond of dogs, had that situation obtained.

In fact we need not flatly reject the standard theory, we may accept a relativized interpretation of it. For a second example of such a relativization of the standard theory consider the following important passage from Kripke 1971, a passage that gives a simple test that is designed to discriminate between designators that are and designators that are not rigid.

> ...we can perfectly well talk about rigid and nonrigid designators. Moreover, we have a simple, intuitive test for them. We can say, for example, that the number of planets might have been a different number from the number it in fact is. For example, there might have been only seven planets. We can say that the inventor of bifocals might have been someone other than the man who *in fact* invented bifocals. We cannot say, though, that the square root of 81 might have been a different number from the number it in fact is, for that number just has to be 9. If we apply this intuitive test to proper names, such as for example 'Richard Nixon', they would seem intuitively to come out to be rigid designators. First, when we talk even about the counterfactual situation in which we suppose Nixon to have done different things, we assume we are still talking about Nixon himself. We say, "If Nixon had bribed a certain Senator, he would have gotten Carswell through", and we assume that by 'Nixon' and 'Carswell' we are still referring to the very same people as in the actual world. And it seems that we cannot say "Nixon might have been a different man from the man he in fact was"...

So the test that tells us whether a designator D is rigid is: Ask whether the thing that is in fact D might not have been D. If the answer is yes, then D is nonrigid; if it is no, then D is rigid.

Now does this test test for the absolute or for the relative version of rigidity? I say it tests for relative rigidity since the 'might' operator that is so crucial in it quantifies only over accessible situations.[5] We cannot draw conclusions about situations that are outside its domain. Again, the quoted passage can be accepted as a whole, provided that we interpret it in a relativized way.

The difference between our theory and the standard one is easily stated: while the accessibility relation ρ is standardly taken to be universal, we do

---

[5]Kripke's 'If Nixon had bribed a certain Senator, he would have gotten Carswell through' suggests that the quantifying force of counterfactuals should be restricted as well. If this is correct, the treatment of counterfactuals in this respect should be like that of the modals, but unlike that of belief contexts.

not think that it is. Formally, the standard theory accepts, but we reject *Universality*:[6],[7]

(113) $\forall ij\,(\rho ji = \top)$ (Universality)

Let me give an extra argument against *Universality*, one that is based upon direct intuition. The Babylonians pictured the heavens to themselves as containing two different objects, Hesperus and Phosphorus. If we would board our time machines and ask the Babylonian astronomers what exactly their theories were, they would undoubtedly be so cooperative as to provide us with stellar maps on which Hesperus and Phosphorus are drawn in different positions. Since the Babylonians were rational people like ourselves, we may assume that these maps do not contain any inconsistencies. The Babylonian picture of astronomical reality was conceivable, it was not logically impossible. In fact the maps that the astronomers are giving to us are (partial) models of reality; incorrect models to be sure, but models nevertheless. They are epistemically possible situations. It seems entirely legitimate to use these maps in a description of the Babylonian beliefs; we need situations corresponding to them in our models if we are to give an adequate account of the semantics of belief sentences. But on the other hand, assuming that a situation in which Hesperus is not equal to Phosphorus is not metaphysically possible, the maps are metaphysically impossible. They are not only wrong in the sense that they do not describe the astronomical facts as they really are; they are impossible in the sense that the actual facts *could not* have been as they describe it. So, while we need the maps in our models, we cannot take them to be metaphysically accessible from the actual situation; they are conceivable situations that cannot be realized.

Let me summarize this chapter briefly. In its first half I have restated a version of the Fregean argument against the Mill-Kripke theory of names. I have argued that a strictly Millian view is incompatible with two minimal assumptions about semantics: if semantics is to be Millian we must either give up Leibniz's Law or cease to take the judgements of language-speakers seriously; we can of course do neither. In the second half of the chapter I have defended Russell's description theory of the logic of ordinary names against Kripke's attack. In defending the theory I had to shed some of its dead weight. In particular I have accepted Kripke's distinction between the description theory of meaning and the description theory of reference and I have dropped the latter; I have also accepted Quine's little modification of the theory. The result, when properly formalized, gives rise to a semantic

---

[6]We have also switched from *Total Function* to *Partial Function*, but this is inessential.

[7]Remember that we are interpreting the necessity operator in its narrow sense, ρ is metaphysical accessibility here. For the wide interpretation I accept *Universality*, but reject *Relative Rigidity*.

theory that is weaker than the standard one and that evades the paradoxes. If this minimal theory is modified slightly (by relativizing the modals and accepting *Relative Rigidity*), we obtain a theory that seems to account for the intuitions behind the Millian view (since it is a relativized version of the standard theory), while it is still compatible with Russell's solution.

Appendix

Proof of Theorem 1

Theorem 1. *Let Γ and Δ be sets of (TT_2) sentences then*

$$\Gamma \models_s \Delta \text{ in } TT_2 \text{ iff } \Gamma \models_s \Delta \text{ in } TY_2.$$

Proof. Let $F = \{D_\alpha \mid \alpha \text{ is a type}\}$ be a standard frame and let $F' = \{D'_\alpha \mid \alpha \text{ is a } TY_2 \text{ type}\}$ be the TY_2 standard frame such that $D_e = D'_e$ and $D_s = D'_s$. Let I be an interpretation function for the frame F and let I' be an interpretation function for F' such that $I'(c) = S_\alpha(I(c))$ for all TT_2 constants c of type α. I'll suppress subscripts on S in the rest of the proof. Let $M = \langle F, I \rangle$ and $M' = \langle F', I' \rangle$. Then, for all TT_2 terms A and all assignments a for M and a' for M' such that $a'(x) = S(a(x))$ for all TT_2 variables x, we have $|A|^{M',a'} = S(\|A\|^{M,a})$, as can be seen by an induction on the complexity of A (I'll sometimes write $|A|$ for $|A|^{M',a'}$, just as I write $\|A\|$ for $\|A\|^{M,a}$, to avoid too much mathematical clutter).

  i. $S(\|c\|) = S(I(c)) = I'(c)$ if c is a constant;
     $S(\|x\|) = S(a(x)) = a'(x)$ if x is a variable;

 ii. Since $S_{()}$ is the identity function on $\{0,1\}$ it holds that
     $S(\|\neg\varphi\|) = 1 - S(\|\varphi\|) = 1 - |\varphi| = |\neg\varphi|$ and that
     $S(\|\varphi \wedge \psi\|) = S(\|\varphi\|) \cap S(\|\psi\|) = |\varphi| \cap |\psi| = |\varphi \wedge \psi|$;

iii.

$$\begin{aligned}
S(\|\forall x_\alpha\, \varphi\|^{M,a}) &= \bigcap_{d \in D_\alpha} S(\|\varphi\|^{M,a[d/x]}) \\
&= \bigcap_{d \in D_\alpha} |\varphi|^{M',a'[S(d)/x]} \\
&= \bigcap_{d' \in D'_{\Sigma(\alpha)}} |\varphi|^{M',a'[d'/x]} \\
&= |\forall x\, \varphi|^{M',a'};
\end{aligned}$$

iv.

$$\begin{aligned}
S(\|AB\|) &= S(F^1_{\|A\|})(\|B\|)) \\
&= S(F^1_{\|A\|}(S^{-1}(|B|^{M',a'})))
\end{aligned}$$

115

$$= S(\|A\|)(|B|)$$
$$= |A|(|B|) = |AB|;$$

v. Since $\|\lambda x_\beta A\|^{M,a}$ is the relation R such that for all $d \in D_\beta$:

$$F_R^1(d) = \|A\|^{M,a[d/x]},$$

$S(\|\lambda x_\beta A\|^{M,a})$ is the function G such that for all $d' \in D'_{\Sigma(\beta)}$:

$$G(d') = S(F_R^1)(S^{-1}(d')) = S(\|A\|^{M,a[d/x]}),$$

where $d = S^{-1}(d')$. So for each $d' \in D'_{\Sigma(\beta)}$,

$$G(d') = |A|^{M',a'[d'/x]}$$

and hence

$$S(\|\lambda x A\|^{M,a}) = |\lambda x A|^{M',a'};$$

vi. $S(\|A = B\|) = 1$ iff $\|A\| = \|B\|$ iff $S(\|A\|) = S(\|B\|)$ iff $|A| = |B|$ iff $|A = B| = 1$.

Now let M be a TT_2 model such that all $\psi \in \Gamma$ are true in M but φ is false in M. Then all $\psi \in \Gamma$ are true in M' as constructed above but φ is false in M'. So if $\Gamma \models \varphi$ in TY_2 then $\Gamma \models \varphi$ in TT_2. Conversely, let $M' = \langle \{D'_\alpha\}_\alpha, I' \rangle$ be a TY_2 model such that all $\psi \in \Gamma$ are true in M' but φ is false in M'. Let $M = \langle \{D_\alpha\}_\alpha, I \rangle$, where $D_e = D'_e$, $D_s = D'_s$ and I is defined as the interpretation function such that $I(c) = S^{-1}(I'(c))$ for all constants c. Then all $\psi \in \Gamma$ are true in M but φ is false in M. So if $\Gamma \models \varphi$ in TT_2 then $\Gamma \models \varphi$ in TY_2. $\square$

Proof of Theorem 2

Theorem 2. *Let Γ and Δ be sets of IL formulae; let $\Gamma^\bullet$ and $\Delta^\bullet$ be the sets $\{\varphi^\bullet \mid \varphi \in \Gamma\}$ and $\{\varphi^\bullet \mid \varphi \in \Delta\}$ respectively, then:*

$$\Gamma \models_s \Delta \text{ in IL} \Leftrightarrow \Gamma^\bullet, \mathrm{AX1}, \dots, \mathrm{AX8} \models_s \Gamma^\bullet \text{ in } TY_2.$$

Proof. Let $M = \langle F, I \rangle$ be a TY_2 standard model satisfying AX1, $\dots$, AX8. We'll prove that M is isomorphic to a TY_2 standard model M' that has a type s domain consisting of a Cartesian product of two sets, the second of which is linearly ordered. Let $F = \{D_\alpha\}_\alpha$, so that its type s domain is D_s. Define $\approx_w$ as $\{\langle d, d' \rangle \mid d, d' \in D_s$ and $I(\approx)(d)(d') = 0\}$ and $\approx_t$ as $\{\langle d, d' \rangle \mid d, d' \in D_s, I(<)(d)(d') = 0$ and $I(<)(d')(d) = 0\}$, where $\approx$ and $<$ are the special type $(s(st))$ constants occurring in the axioms. Both relations are equivalence relations; in case of $\approx_w$ this follows trivially from AX1, $\dots$, AX3, in case of $\approx_t$ it follows from AX4 and AX6 by elementary reasoning. Define for each $d \in D_s$ the equivalence class $[d]_w$ as $\{d' \in D_s \mid d \approx_w d'\}$ and define $[d]_t$ as $\{d' \in D_s \mid d \approx_t d'\}$. Define $W = \{[d]_w \mid d \in D_s\}$ and $T = \{[d]_t \mid d \in D_s\}$ and stipulate that $[d]_t <_t [d']_t$ iff $I(<)(d)(d') = 1$. Use AX4 and AX6 again to see that the last definition is correct and use AX4 and AX5 to see that $<_t$ is a strict linear ordering of T.

The function ι, given by $\iota(d) = \langle [d]_w, [d]_t \rangle$, is a bijection from D_s onto $W \times T$. To see that it is surjective use AX7 and to see that it is injective use AX8. Let $F' = \{D'_\alpha\}_\alpha$ be the TY_2 standard frame such that $D'_e = D_e$ and $D'_s = W \times T$. We'll define bijections $\iota_\alpha : D_\alpha \to D'_\alpha$ by induction on α. If α is a basic type other than s let ι_α be the identity function, let $\iota_s = \iota$ and let $\iota_{(\alpha\beta)}$ be the function such that for each $f \in D_{(\alpha\beta)}$ and for each $d \in D'_\alpha : \iota_{(\alpha\beta)}(f)(d) = \iota_\beta(f(\iota_\alpha^{-1}(d)))$. Define the interpretation function I' by $I'(c_\alpha) = \iota_\alpha(I(c_\alpha))$ and let $M' = \langle F', I' \rangle$. If a is an assignment function for M let a' be the assignment function for M' defined by $a'(x_\alpha) = \iota_\alpha(a(x_\alpha))$. A straightforward induction on term complexity now shows that $|A|^{M',a'} = \iota_\alpha(|A|^{M,a})$ for each TY_2 term A and hence that $|\varphi|^{M',a'} = |\varphi|^{M,a}$ for each formula φ.

Now suppose that some TY_2 standard model $M = \langle F, I \rangle$ and an assignment a for M satisfy $\Gamma^\bullet$ and the axioms AX1, ..., AX8 but fail to satisfy a formula in $\Delta^\bullet$. From the above considerations we may deduce that we may assume without loss of generality that M's s-type domain D_s equals a Cartesian product $W \times T$ and that T is linearly ordered by $<_t$. Moreover we may assume that $I(\approx)(\langle w, t \rangle)(\langle w', t' \rangle) = 1$ iff $w = w'$ and that $I(<)(\langle w, t \rangle)(\langle w', t' \rangle) = 1$ iff $t <_t t'$. We'll define an IL model M' and an assignment a' such that Γ is satisfied but no $d \in D$ is. Let $I'(c) = I(k)$ where k is the n-th constant of IL type $(s\alpha)$ if c is the n-th constant of type a and let $M' = \langle D, W, T, <_t, I' \rangle$ (where D is M's e-type domain). Let i be the type s variable that occurs free in translations of IL formulae and let $\langle w, t \rangle = a(i)$; let a' be the restriction of a to IL variables. By a straightforward induction on the complexity of IL terms we find that for each IL term A: $\|A\|^{M',w,t,a'} = |A^\bullet|^{M,a}$. Hence M' and a' satisfy Γ but do not satisfy a $\delta \in \Delta$.

Now conversely let $M' = \langle D, W, T, <_t, I' \rangle$ be an IL model and let a' be an assignment for M' such that M' and a' satisfy all formulae in Γ but no formula in Δ. Let $F = \{D_\alpha\}_\alpha$ be the standard TY_2 frame such that $D_s = D$ and $D_s = W \times T$. Let $I(\approx)(\langle w, t \rangle)(\langle w', t' \rangle) = 1$ iff $w = w'$ and $I(<)(\langle w, t \rangle)(\langle w', t' \rangle) = 1$ iff $t <_t t'$; let $I(k) = I'(c)$ where c is the n-th constant of IL type a if k is the n-th constant of type $(s\alpha)$ (without loss of generality we assume that the special constants $<$ and $\approx$ fall outside the fixed numbering of TY_2 constants) and let $I(k)$ be an arbitrary element of D_α if k is any other constant of any type α. Let $M = \langle F, I \rangle$. Clearly M is a standard TY_2 model that satisfies AX1, ..., AX8. Let a be an arbitrary extension to TY_2 variables of a' and again let $\langle w, t \rangle = a(i)$. Again we find that $\|A\|^{M',w,t,a'} = |A^\bullet|^{M,a}$, which proves the theorem. $\square$

Proof of Theorem 3

Theorem 3. *For each analysis tree ξ let ξ' be the translation it is given in DWP. Let Δ be a set of DWP meaning postulates, to be specified below, and let $\Xi \cup \{\vartheta\}$ be a set of analysis trees, then:*

$$\Xi^\circ \models_{AX} \vartheta^\circ \text{ in } TT_2 \quad \text{iff} \quad \Xi', \Delta \models \vartheta' \text{ in } IL.$$

Proof. In order to give content to this theorem we must specify the DWP translation function ' and the set of meaning postulates Δ. We begin with the latter. Let G be a variable of type $s(e((s(et))(et)))$ and let S be a variable of type $s(e(et))$. Δ will be the following set of IL sentences:

  (i) $\exists x \Box\, (x = c)$, where c is any constant of type e;

  (ii) $\exists S \forall x \forall Q \Box\, (\delta Q x \leftrightarrow (\check{}Q)\hat{}\lambda y\,((\check{}S)yx))$, where δ is find$'$, love$'$, lose$'$, eat$'$ or date$'$;

  (iii) $\exists G \forall Q \forall P \forall x \Box(\text{in}'QPx \leftrightarrow (\check{}Q)\hat{}\lambda y\,((\check{}G)yPx))$.

The translation function ' as it is employed in DWP is defined below.

Definition. (DWP Translations) Let g be some fixed one-to-one function having the set of basic expressions other than those mentioned explicitly in rule $T1'$ below as its domain, such that $g(\xi)$ is an IL constant of type $f(A)$ (defined in Table 1) if ξ is of category A. For each analysis tree ξ define its *DWP translation* ξ' by induction on the complexity of analysis trees:

T1'.   If ξ is in the domain of g then $\xi' = g(\xi)$;
         John$' = \lambda P(\check{}P john_e)$, Mary$' = \lambda P(\check{}P mary_e)$,
         Bill$' = \lambda P(\check{}P bill_e)$,
         he$'_n = \lambda P(\check{}P x_n)$;
         be$' = \lambda Q \lambda y\,(\check{}Q\hat{}\lambda x\,(x = y))$;
         every$' = \lambda P_1 \lambda P_2 \forall x\,(\check{}P_1 x \rightarrow \check{}P_2 x)$,
         a$' = \lambda P_1 \lambda P_2 \exists x\,(\check{}P_1 x \wedge \check{}P_2 x)$,
         the$' = \lambda P_1 \lambda P_2 \exists x\,(\forall y\,(\check{}P_1 y \leftrightarrow x = y) \wedge \check{}P_2 x)$;
         necessarily$' = \lambda p \Box(\check{}p)$;

T2'. $([\xi\vartheta]^{2,n})' = \lambda x_n(\xi'(x_n) \wedge \vartheta')$

T3'–T10'. $([\xi\vartheta]^k)' = \xi'(\hat{}\vartheta')$ if $3 \leq k \leq 10$;

T11'. $([\xi\vartheta]^{11a})' = \xi' \wedge \vartheta'$;
         $([\xi\vartheta]^{11b})' = \xi' \vee \vartheta'$;

T12'. $([\xi\vartheta]^{12a})' = \lambda x\,(\xi'(x) \wedge \vartheta'(x))$;
         $([\xi\vartheta]^{12b})' = \lambda x\,(\xi'(x) \vee \vartheta'(x))$;

T13'. $([\xi\vartheta]^{13})' = \lambda P\,(\xi'(P) \vee \vartheta'(P))$;

T14'. $([\xi\vartheta]^{14,n})' = \xi'(\hat{}\lambda x_n \vartheta')$;

T15'. $([\xi\vartheta]^{15,n})' = \lambda y\,(\xi'(\lambda x_n(\vartheta'(y))))$;

T16'. $([\xi\vartheta]^{16,n})' = \lambda y\,(\xi'(\lambda x_n(\vartheta'(y))))$;

T17'. $([\xi\vartheta]^{17})' = \neg\xi'(\hat{}\vartheta')$.

We can now start with the proof proper. Using Theorem 2 we find that $\Xi' \models_s \vartheta'$ in IL if and only if $\Xi'^\bullet, \mathrm{AX} \models_s \vartheta'^\bullet$ in TY_2. If A is an IL term then $A^\clubsuit$ will denote the result of replacing each subterm of $A^\bullet$ that is of the form ki, where k is the n-th individual constant of type (se), with the n-th individual of type e. Let Θ be the set of all IL formula of the form $\exists x \,\Box(x = c)$, where c is a constant of type e, then clearly $\Xi', \Theta \models_s \vartheta'$ in IL if and only if $\Xi'^\clubsuit, \mathrm{AX} \models_s \vartheta'^\clubsuit$ in TY_2. By an easy induction on the complexity of analysis trees we verify that for each tree ξ the TY_2 term $\xi'^\clubsuit$ is in fact a TT_2 term: none of its subterms will have a type in which an e or an s immediately precedes a right parenthesis. So in virtue of Theorem 1 we have that $\Xi', \Theta \models_s \vartheta'$ in IL if and only if $\Xi'^\clubsuit \models_{\mathrm{AX}} \vartheta'^\clubsuit$ in TT_2.

But in general $\xi'^\clubsuit$ will not be equivalent to ξ°; the types will not match. The main reason for this is that our category-to-type rule places s's immediately before right brackets, while in the type of any $\lambda i\,(\xi'^\clubsuit)$ these s's occupy a place immediately following the corresponding left brackets. So we have to permute types.

Definition. Define, for each α, the type $\alpha^\blacklozenge$ by:

I $e^\blacklozenge = e$; $s^\blacklozenge = s$;

II i. $\langle\rangle^\blacklozenge = \langle\rangle$

ii. $\langle \alpha_1 \ldots \alpha_n \alpha_{n+1} \rangle^\blacklozenge = \langle \alpha_{n+1}^\blacklozenge \alpha_1^\blacklozenge \ldots \alpha_n^\blacklozenge \rangle$

And we embed TT_2 in itself.

Definition. Define for each TT_2 term A of type α a TT_2 term $A^\heartsuit$ of type $\alpha^\blacklozenge$ by the following induction.

i. $c^\heartsuit = k$, where k is the n-th constant of type $\alpha^\blacklozenge$ in some fixed ordering, if c is the n-th constant of type α;

$x^\heartsuit = y$, where y is the n-th variable of type $\alpha^\blacklozenge$ in some fixed ordering, if x is the n-th variable of type α;

ii. $(\neg\varphi)^\heartsuit = \neg\varphi^\heartsuit$;

$(\varphi \wedge \psi)^\heartsuit = \varphi^\heartsuit \wedge \psi^\heartsuit$;

iii. $(\forall x\,\varphi)^\heartsuit = \forall x^\heartsuit \, \varphi^\heartsuit$;

iv. $(A_{\langle \beta \rangle} B_\beta)^\heartsuit = A^\heartsuit B^\heartsuit$,

$(A_{\langle \beta \alpha_1 \ldots \alpha_{n+1} \rangle} B_\beta)^\heartsuit = \lambda x\,(A^\heartsuit x B^\heartsuit)$, where x is the first variable of type $\alpha_{n+1}^\blacklozenge$ that does not occur free in $A^\heartsuit$ or $B^\heartsuit$;

v. $(\lambda x\,\varphi_{\langle\rangle})^\heartsuit = (\lambda x^\heartsuit \, \varphi^\heartsuit)$,

$(\lambda x_\beta A_{\langle \alpha_1 \ldots \alpha_{n+1} \rangle})^\heartsuit = \lambda y \lambda x^\heartsuit (A^\heartsuit y)$, where y is the first variable of type $\alpha_{n+1}^\blacklozenge$ that does not occur free in $A^\heartsuit$;

vi. $(A = B)^\heartsuit = A^\heartsuit = B^\heartsuit$.

We prove that $^\heartsuit$ preserves entailment. Let $M = \langle \{D_\alpha\}_\alpha, I \rangle$ be a model and let a be an assignment for it. Define $\pi(d) = d$ if $d \in D_e$, $d \in D_s$ or

$d \in D_{()}$ and define

$$\pi(R) = \{\langle \pi(d_{n+1}), \pi(d_1), \ldots, \pi(d_n)\rangle \mid \langle d_1, \ldots, d_n, d_{n+1}\rangle \in R\}$$

if $R \in D_{\langle \alpha_1 \ldots \alpha_n \alpha_{n+1}\rangle}$. It is easily seen that the restriction of π to D_α is a bijection between D_α and D_α. Let I' be an interpretation function such that $I'(c^{\heartsuit}) = \pi(I(c))$ for all constants c. Define $M' := \langle \{D_\alpha\}_\alpha, I'\rangle$. Then by an induction on term complexity that we leave to the reader: $\|A^{\heartsuit}\|^{M', a'} = \pi(\|A\|^{M, a})$ if a' is an assignment such that $a'(x^{\heartsuit}) = \pi(a(x))$, for all variables x. It readily follows that $\Gamma \models \Delta$ if and only if $\Gamma^{\heartsuit} \models \Delta^{\heartsuit}$.

Note that if A is an $n+1$-ary term then $(AB_1 \ldots B_n B_{n+1})^{\heartsuit}$ is equivalent to $A^{\heartsuit} B_{n+1}^{\heartsuit} B_1^{\heartsuit} \ldots B_n^{\heartsuit}$. Also note that $(\lambda x_1 \ldots \lambda x_n \lambda x_{n+1} \, \varphi_{()})^{\heartsuit}$ is equivalent to $\lambda x_{n+1}^{\heartsuit} \lambda x_1^{\heartsuit} \ldots \lambda x_n^{\heartsuit} \varphi_{()}$.

Let $\spadesuit$ be a function from analysis trees to TT_2 terms that is defined just as $\circ$ is, with the exception that $\text{find}^{\spadesuit}$, $\text{love}^{\spadesuit}$, $\text{lose}^{\spadesuit}$, $\text{eat}^{\spadesuit}$, $\text{date}^{\spadesuit}$, and $\text{in}^{\spadesuit}$ are all constants (of the appropriate type) instead of complex logical expressions. Let Ω be the following set of terms:

$$\lambda j \exists S_{\langle ees\rangle} \forall x \forall Q \, (\delta Q x = Q \lambda y \, (Syx)),$$

where δ is $\text{find}^{\spadesuit}$, $\text{love}^{\spadesuit}$, $\text{lose}^{\spadesuit}$, $\text{eat}^{\spadesuit}$ or $\text{date}^{\spadesuit}$;

$$\lambda j \exists G_{\langle e\langle es\rangle es\rangle} \forall Q \forall P \forall x \, (\text{in}^{\spadesuit} Q P x = Q \lambda y \, (GyPx)).$$

Clearly, $\Xi^{\circ} \models \vartheta^{\circ} \Leftrightarrow \Xi^{\spadesuit}, \Omega \models \vartheta^{\spadesuit}$.

Without loss of generality we may assume that if δ is any basic expression of category A other than the ones mentioned explicitly in clause T1$'$ of the definition of $'$ above, then δ' is the n-th IL constant of type $f(A)$ if and only if $\delta^{\spadesuit}$ is the n-th TT_2 constant of type $\tau(A)$. We can now bridge the gap between the DWP translation and ours.

Lemma. $\lambda i \, (\xi'^{\spadesuit})$ (where i is the variable in Gallin's Embedding) is equivalent to $\xi^{\spadesuit \heartsuit}$ for all analysis trees ξ.

The proof is a straightforward but tedious induction on the complexity of analysis trees which I leave to the reader.

Combining our findings thus far, we see that

$$\Xi', \Theta \models_s \vartheta' \text{ in IL}$$
$$\Leftrightarrow \quad \Xi'^{\spadesuit} \models_{\text{AX}} \vartheta'^{\spadesuit} \text{ in TT}_2$$
$$\Leftrightarrow \quad \{\lambda i \, (\xi'^{\spadesuit}) \mid \xi \in \Xi\} \models_{\text{AX}} \lambda i \, (\vartheta'^{\spadesuit})$$
$$\Leftrightarrow \quad \Xi^{\spadesuit \heartsuit} \models_{\text{AX}} \vartheta^{\spadesuit \heartsuit}$$
$$\Leftrightarrow \quad \Xi^{\spadesuit} \models_{\text{AX}} \vartheta^{\spadesuit}.$$

Since it can easily be verified that for each $\varphi \in \Omega$ there is an $A \in \Delta - \Theta$ such that $\lambda i \, (\varphi^{\spadesuit})$ is equivalent to $A^{\heartsuit}$ and vice versa, we see that

$$\Xi', \Delta \models_s \vartheta' \text{ in IL} \Leftrightarrow \Xi^{\spadesuit}, \Omega \models_{\text{AX}} \vartheta^{\spadesuit} \Leftrightarrow \Xi^{\circ} \models_{\text{AX}} \vartheta^{\circ},$$

which proves the theorem. $\qquad \square$

Proof of Theorem 4

Theorem 4. *Every truth function is expressed by some formula.*

Proof. The proof proceeds by induction on the arity of truth functions. The formulae $\star$, $\#$, $\top$ and $\bot$ express the zero-place truth functions. Let $f : \{\mathbf{T}, \mathbf{F}, \mathbf{N}, \mathbf{B}\}^{n+1} \to \{\mathbf{T}, \mathbf{F}, \mathbf{N}, \mathbf{B}\}$ be an $n+1$-ary truth function. Define for each $x_1, \ldots, x_n \in \{\mathbf{T}, \mathbf{F}, \mathbf{N}, \mathbf{B}\}$:

$$
\begin{aligned}
f_1(x_1, \ldots, x_n) &= f(x_1, \ldots, x_n, \mathbf{T}) \\
f_2(x_1, \ldots, x_n) &= f(x_1, \ldots, x_n, \mathbf{F}) \\
f_3(x_1, \ldots, x_n) &= f(x_1, \ldots, x_n, \mathbf{N}) \\
f_4(x_1, \ldots, x_n) &= f(x_1, \ldots, x_n, \mathbf{B})
\end{aligned}
$$

Using the induction hypothesis we find that there are formulae φ_1, φ_2, φ_3 and φ_4, containing exactly the propositional constants $p_1, \ldots, p_n$ such that $\|\varphi_i\|^V = f_i(V(p_1), \ldots, V(p_n))$ for each valuation function V. Let φ be the formula

$$
((p_{n+1} = \top) \to \varphi_1) \wedge ((p_{n+1} = \bot) \to \varphi_2) \wedge ((p_{n+1} = \star) \to \varphi_3) \wedge
$$
$$
((p_{n+1} = \#) \to \varphi_4).
$$

Clearly $\|\varphi\|^V = f(V(p_1), \ldots, V(p_{n+1}))$ for each V and φ contains exactly the propositional constants $p_1, \ldots, p_{n+1}$, so φ expresses f and the proposition is proved. $\qquad\square$

Proof of Theorem 5

Theorem 5. *A truth function is monotonic if and only if it is expressed by a sentence that is built up from propositional constants using only $\star$, $\#$, $\wedge$, $\neg$ and $\top$.*

Proof. An easy induction on sentences that are built up from propositional constants with the help of $\star$, $\#$, $\wedge$, $\neg$ and $\top$ shows that such sentences express only monotonic truth functions. So let f be an n-ary monotonic truth function. For each n-ary sequence $x_1, \ldots, x_n \in \{\mathbf{T}, \mathbf{F}, \mathbf{N}, \mathbf{B}\}$ and for each number i such that $1 \leq i \leq n$ we define formulae $t^i_{\langle x_1, \ldots, x_n \rangle}$ and $f^i_{\langle x_1, \ldots, x_n \rangle}$ in the following way.

If $f(x_1, \ldots, x_n)$ includes truth:

$$
\begin{aligned}
t^i_{\langle x_1, \ldots, x_n \rangle} &= p_i & \text{if } x_i = \mathbf{T} \\
&= \neg p_i & \text{if } x_i = \mathbf{F} \\
&= p_i \wedge \neg p_i & \text{if } x_i = \mathbf{B} \\
&= \top & \text{if } x_i = \mathbf{N}
\end{aligned}
$$

$t^i_{\langle x_1, \ldots, x_n \rangle} = \bot$ otherwise.

If $f(x_1, \ldots, x_n)$ includes falsity:

$$
\begin{aligned}
f^i_{\langle x_1, \ldots, x_n \rangle} &= \neg p_i & \text{if } x_i = \mathbf{T} \\
&= p_i & \text{if } x_i = \mathbf{F} \\
&= p_i \vee \neg p_i & \text{if } x_i = \mathbf{B} \\
&= \bot & \text{if } x_i = \mathbf{N}
\end{aligned}
$$

$f^i_{\langle x_1, \ldots, x_n \rangle} = \top$ otherwise.

Let φ be the formula

$$
\left[\bigvee_{\langle x_1, \ldots, x_n \rangle} \bigwedge_i t^i_{\langle x_1, \ldots, x_n \rangle} \right] @ \left[\bigwedge_{\langle x_1, \ldots, x_n \rangle} \bigvee_i f^i_{\langle x_1, \ldots, x_n \rangle} \right]
$$

In view of the eliminability of $\vee$, $\bot$ and @ the formula φ can be said to be built up with the help of $\star$, $\#$, $\wedge$, $\neg$ and $\top$ only. We'll show that φ expresses f. Remember that a formula of the form $\chi @ \psi$ has the truth conditions of χ but the falsity conditions of ψ: its value includes truth iff χ's value includes truth, it includes falsity iff ψ's value includes falsity.

Let V be an arbitrary valuation. It follows from the definition of φ that if $f(V(p_1), \ldots, V(p_n))$ includes truth (falsity), $\|\varphi\|^V$ includes truth (falsity) as well. To prove the converse, suppose $\|\varphi\|^V$ includes truth. Then there are $x_1, \ldots, x_n$ such that (a) $\|t^i_{\langle x_1, \ldots, x_n \rangle}\|^V$ includes truth for all i ($1 \le i \le n$) and (b) $f(x_1, \ldots, x_n)$ includes truth. By inspection of φ's definition we see that $x_i \sqsubseteq V(p_i)$ for all i. (Suppose, for example, that $x_i = \mathbf{F}$. Then $t^i_{\langle x_1, \ldots, x_n \rangle} = \neg p_i$ and since the value of this formula includes truth, $V(p_i)$ must equal $\mathbf{F}$ or $\mathbf{B}$. But $\mathbf{F} \sqsubseteq \mathbf{F}$ and $\mathbf{F} \sqsubseteq \mathbf{B}$, hence $x_i \sqsubseteq V(p_i)$. The other cases go similarly.) That $f(V(p_1), \ldots, V(p_n))$ includes truth now follows by the monotonicity of f. In a completely analogous fashion we find that $f(V(p_1), \ldots, V(p_n))$ includes falsity if $\|\varphi\|^V$ includes falsity. Conclusion: $\|\varphi\|^V = f(V(p_1), \ldots, V(p_n))$ for arbitrary valuations V and φ expresses f. $\qquad\square$

Proofs of Theorem 6 and corollaries

Theorem 6. *Let Γ and Δ be sets of sentences of partial predicate logic. Define $\Gamma^\dagger$ to be the set $\{\varphi^\dagger \mid \varphi \in \Gamma\}$ and similarly define $\Delta^\dagger$ to be $\{\psi^\dagger \mid \psi \in D\}$. Write $\models_2$ for the relation of entailment in predicate logic. Then:*

$$
\Gamma \models \Delta \text{ iff } \Gamma^\dagger, (p^+ \wedge \neg p^-) \vee (p^- \wedge \neg p^+) \models_2 \Delta^\dagger.
$$

Proof. We prove the following:

   i. $\Gamma \models \Delta, \star$ iff $\Gamma^\dagger, p^+ \wedge \neg p^- \models_2 \Delta^\dagger$

   ii. $\Gamma, \star \models \Delta$ iff $\Gamma^\dagger, p^- \wedge \neg p^+ \models_2 \Delta^\dagger$.

Since $\Gamma \models \Delta$ is equivalent to the conjunction of $\Gamma \models \Delta, \star$ and $\Gamma, \star \models \Delta$ the desired conclusion then readily follows.

i. Suppose $\Gamma \models \Delta, \star$ does not hold; then there is some model $M_4 = \langle D, I^+, I^- \rangle$ such that $M_4 \models \varphi$ for all $\varphi \in \Gamma$ but $M_4 \models \psi$ for no $\psi \in \Delta$. Define the two-valued interpretation I_2 by clauses (i.), (ii.) and (iii.) in the Embedding Lemma. Let $M_2 = \langle D, I_2 \rangle$. We have $M_2 \models \sigma$ for all sentences $\sigma \in G^\dagger$, $p^+ \wedge \neg p^-$ but $M_2 \models \psi$ for no $\psi^\dagger \in \Delta^\dagger$; hence it does not hold that $\Gamma^\dagger, p^+ \wedge \neg p^- \models_2 \Delta^\dagger$.

Now suppose conversely that $\Gamma^\dagger, p^+ \wedge \neg p^- \models_2 \Delta^\dagger$ fails. There is a model M_2 for $\Gamma^\dagger$ and $p^+ \wedge \neg p^-$ that does not satisfy any of the sentences in $\Delta^\dagger$. Let $I^+(c) = I^-(c) = I_2(c)$ for each individual constant $c \in L$, let $I^+(R) = I_2(R^+)$ and let $I^-(R) = D^n - I_2(R^-)$ for all n-ary relation symbols R. Define $M_4 = \langle D, I^+, I^- \rangle$ then clearly M_2 and M_4 are related as in the Embedding Lemma. So we have $M_4 \models \varphi$ for all $\varphi \in \Gamma$ but $M_4 \models \psi$ for no $\psi \in \Delta$, from which it follows that $\Gamma \models \Delta, \star$ does not hold.

ii. Since $\Gamma, \star \models \Delta$ if and only if $\{\neg \psi \mid \psi \in \Delta\} \models \{\neg \varphi \mid \varphi \in \Gamma\}, \star$ it follows from i. that $\Gamma, \star \models \Delta$ iff $\{\neg \pm \psi^\dagger \mid \psi \in \Delta\}, p^+ \wedge \neg p^- \models_2 \{\neg \pm \varphi^\dagger \mid \varphi \in \Gamma\}$. A simultaneous substitution shows that this in its turn is equivalent to $\{\neg \psi^\dagger \mid \psi \in \Delta\}, p^- \wedge \neg p^+ \models_2 \{\neg \varphi^\dagger \mid \varphi \in \Gamma\}$, whence we have that $\Gamma, \star \models \Delta$ iff $\Gamma^\dagger, p^- \wedge \neg p^+ \models_2 \Delta^\dagger$. $\qquad \square$

Corollary. (Compactness Theorem for partial predicate logic) *If every finite subset of some theory has a model then that theory has a model.*

Proof. Suppose that every finite $\Sigma_0 \subseteq \Sigma$ has some model M_4'. By the reasoning above for every finite $\Sigma_0 \subseteq \Sigma$ we can find a two-valued model M_2' such that $M_2' \models \Sigma_0^\dagger, p^+ \wedge \neg p^-$. Hence by the compactness theorem for predicate logic $\Sigma^\dagger \cup \{p^+ \wedge \neg p^-\}$ has a two-valued model M_2. Define a model M_4 for partial predicate logic from M_2 as above; then $M_4 \models \Sigma$. $\qquad \square$

Corollary. (Löwenheim-Skolem Theorem for partial predicate logic) *If a theory has an infinite model then it has a countably infinite model.*

Proof. Suppose that M_4 is an infinite model for Σ. We can find an infinite M_2 such that $M_2 \models \Sigma^\dagger, p^+ \wedge \neg p^-$; hence for some countably infinite M_2' it holds that $M_2' \models \Sigma^\dagger, p^+ \wedge \neg p^-$. From M_2' we find a countably infinite M_4' such that $M_4' \models \Sigma$. $\qquad \square$

Corollary. *There is a recursive axiomatization of partial predicate logic.*

Proof. It suffices to prove that $\{\varphi \mid \models \varphi\}$ is recursively enumerable. But this follows from the recursive axiomatizability of standard predicate logic and the fact that the embedding function † clearly is recursive. $\qquad \square$

Corollary. *Let* Γ *and* Δ *be sets of sentences of partial predicate logic that are built up from* $\neg, \wedge, \top, \bot, =$ *and* $\forall$. *Then* $\Gamma \models \Delta, \star$ *iff* $\Gamma, \star \models \Delta$.

Proof. The †-translations of such sentences do not contain the zero place relation symbols p^+ and p^-. Hence $\Gamma \models \Delta, \star$ iff $\Gamma^\dagger, \models_2 \Delta^\dagger$ iff $\Gamma, \star \models \Delta$.

$\square$

Proof of Theorem 7

Theorem 7. (Representation Theorem for Kleene algebras) *Every Kleene algebra is isomorphic to a natural Kleene algebra on a set of partial sets.*

Proof. In distributive lattices with zero and one a *prime filter* can be defined as a set ∇ such that the following hold:

$$a + b \in \nabla \quad \Leftrightarrow \quad a \in \nabla \text{ or } b \in \nabla$$

$$a \cdot b \in \nabla \quad \Leftrightarrow \quad a \in \nabla \text{ and } b \in \nabla$$

$$0 \notin \nabla \qquad 1 \in \nabla.$$

We let ∇ range over prime filters.

Let K be a Kleene algebra. We'll show that there is a natural Kleene algebra, with partial sets of prime filters on K as its elements, that is isomorphic with K. Define a function f with the domain of K as its domain by:

$$f(a) = \langle \{\nabla \mid a \in \nabla\}, \{\nabla \mid a' \in \nabla\} \rangle$$

for each a. Then by Stone's Theorem f is 1-1. Using the properties of prime filters cited above and the axioms of Kleene algebras it is easily verified that moreover f is an isomorphism:

$$
\begin{aligned}
f(a') &= \langle \{\nabla \mid a' \in \nabla\}, \{\nabla \mid a'' \in \nabla\} \rangle \\
&= \langle \{\nabla \mid a' \in \nabla\}, \{\nabla \mid a \in \nabla\} \rangle \\
&= -\langle \{\nabla \mid a \in \nabla\}, \{\nabla \mid a' \in \nabla\} \rangle \\
&= -f(a)
\end{aligned}
$$

$$
\begin{aligned}
f(a + b) &= \langle \{\nabla \mid a + b \in \nabla\}, \{\nabla \mid (a + b)' \in \nabla\} \rangle \\
&= \langle \{\nabla \mid a + b \in \nabla\}, \{\nabla \mid a' \cdot b' \in \nabla\} \rangle \\
&= \langle \{\nabla \mid a \in \nabla \text{ or } b \in \nabla\}, \{\nabla \mid a' \in \nabla \text{ and } b' \in \nabla\} \rangle \\
&= \langle \{\nabla \mid a \in \nabla\}, \{\nabla \mid a' \in \nabla\} \rangle \cup \\
&\qquad \langle \{\nabla \mid b \in \nabla\}, \{\nabla \mid b' \in \nabla\} \rangle \\
&= f(a) \cup f(b)
\end{aligned}
$$

$$f(a \cdot b) = f(a) \cap f(b) \text{ by dual reasoning}$$

$$f(0) \ = \ \langle \{\nabla \mid 0 \in \nabla\}, \{\nabla \mid 1 \in \nabla\}\rangle$$
$$= \ \langle \emptyset, \{\nabla \mid \nabla = \nabla\}\rangle$$

$$f(1) \ = \ \langle \{\nabla \mid 1 \in \nabla\}, \{\nabla \mid 0 \in \nabla\}\rangle$$
$$= \ \langle \{\nabla \mid \nabla = \nabla\}, \emptyset\rangle.$$

$\square$

Proof of Theorem 9

Theorem 9. *Let Π and Σ be sets of formulae then:*

$$\Pi \vdash \Sigma \ \Leftrightarrow \ \Pi \models \Sigma.$$

Proof. Before we can give the proof itself we must state two lemmas about the syntactical consequence relation $\vdash$. The first lemma says that certain formulae behave in a classical way. Its proof is an easy induction.

Lemma 1. *Define a 2-formula to be a formula that is built up from formulae of the form $A = B$ and the logical operators $\neg$, $\wedge$ and $\forall$ solely. If φ is a 2-formula then $\vdash \varphi, \neg\varphi$.*

The second lemma lists some provable sequents that we shall either need below or need in the proof of the lemma itself.

Lemma 2. *Let $T\varphi$ ('φ is true') be an abbreviation of the formula $(\varphi = \top) \vee (\varphi = \#)$. The following sequents are provable.*

I	$\Rightarrow \neg\neg\top$	*(use the negation rules)*
II	$\Rightarrow \neg\neg\top = \top$	*(use I and the Truth-Value rules)*
III	$\Rightarrow \neg\neg\bot = \bot$	*(use II and the definition of $\bot$)*
IV	$\Rightarrow \neg\neg\star = \star$	*(use the Truth-Value rules)*
V	$\Rightarrow \neg\neg\# = \#$	*(use the Truth-Value rules)*
VI	$\Rightarrow \neg\neg\varphi = \varphi$	*(use II, III, IV, V)*
VII	$\varphi = \top \Rightarrow \varphi$	
VIII	$\varphi = \# \Rightarrow \varphi, \star$	*(use the Truth-Value rules)*
IX	$\varphi = \# \Rightarrow \neg\varphi, \star$	*(use VI and VIII)*
X	$\varphi = \star, \varphi \Rightarrow \star$	
XI	$\varphi = \star, \neg\varphi \Rightarrow \star$	*(use VI and X)*
XII	$\varphi = \bot, \varphi \Rightarrow$	*(use the definition of $\bot$)*
XIII	$\varphi = \top, \neg\varphi \Rightarrow$	
XIV	$\varphi = \bot \Rightarrow \neg\varphi$	
XV	$\varphi \Rightarrow \varphi = \top, \varphi = \#, \varphi = \star$	*(use XII)*
XVI	$\varphi \Rightarrow \varphi = \top, \varphi = \#, \star$	*(use X and XV)*

$XVII \quad \Rightarrow \varphi, \neg\varphi, \varphi = \star, \star$ *(use VII, VIII and XIV)*
$XVIII \quad \varphi, \neg\varphi \Rightarrow \varphi = \#, \star$ *(use XIII and XVI)*
$XIX \quad \varphi \Rightarrow \neg\varphi, \varphi = \top, \star$ *(use IX and XVI)*
$XX \quad \neg\varphi \Rightarrow \varphi, \varphi = \bot, \star$ *(use XIX)*
$XXI \quad T\varphi \Rightarrow \varphi, \star$ *(use VII and VIII)*

We now come to the main part of the proof, which is a generalization of the standard Henkin generalized completeness proof for type theory. A set of formulae Γ is called $\star$-*consistent* if it does not hold that $\Gamma \vdash \star$.

Theorem (Star-Consistency Theorem) *If a set of formulae is $\star$-consistent then it has a general model.*

Proof. Let Γ be a $\star$-consistent set of formulae. We construct a general model for Γ. Add denumerably many constants of each type to the language of Γ and let $\varphi_0, \ldots, \varphi_n, \ldots$ be some enumeration of all formulae in the extended language. For each natural number n, define a set of formulae Γ_n by the following induction.

$$\Gamma_0 = \Gamma$$

$$\Gamma_{n+1} = \begin{cases} \Gamma_n, & \text{if } \Gamma_n, \varphi_n \vdash \star \text{ and } \varphi_n \text{ is not of} \\ & \text{the form } \forall x\, \psi \\[4pt] \Gamma_n \cup \{\varphi_n\}, & \text{if } \Gamma_n, \varphi_n \not\vdash \star \text{ and } \varphi_n \text{ is not of} \\ & \text{the form } \neg\forall x\, \psi \\[4pt] \Gamma_n \cup \{\neg T[c/x]\psi\}, & \text{where } c \text{ is the first constant} \\ & \text{of type } \alpha \text{ (in some fixed enu-} \\ & \text{meration) that does not oc-} \\ & \text{cur in any of the sentences in} \\ & \Gamma_n \cup \{\psi\}, \text{ if } \Gamma_n, \varphi_n \vdash \star \text{ and} \\ & \varphi_n \equiv \forall x_\alpha\, \psi \\[4pt] \Gamma_n \cup \{\varphi_n, [c/x]\neg\psi\}, & \text{where } c \text{ is the first constant of} \\ & \text{type } \alpha \text{ that does not occur in} \\ & \text{any of the sentences in } \Gamma_n \cup \\ & \{\psi\} \text{ if } \Gamma_n, \varphi_n \not\vdash \star \text{ and } \varphi_n \equiv \\ & \neg\forall x_\alpha\, \psi. \end{cases}$$

We show by induction that each Γ_n is $\star$-consistent. By assumption Γ_0 is $\star$-consistent. The first two cases in the proof of the induction step are trivial, so let $\Gamma_n, \forall x_\alpha \psi \vdash \star$ and suppose that $\Gamma_n, \neg T[c/x]\psi \vdash \star$. Then since $T[c/x]\psi$ is a 2-formula we have that $\Gamma_n \vdash T[c/x]\psi, \star$, from which it follows that $\Gamma_n \vdash [c/x]\psi, \star$. Since c doesn't occur in Γ_n or ψ we see that $\Gamma_n \vdash \forall x\, \psi, \star$ by IV. By the Cut rule $\Gamma_n \vdash \star$, which contradicts the induction hypothesis. To prove the last step, use IV and the negation rules to see that $\Gamma_n \cup \{\neg\forall x\, \psi, [c/x]\neg\psi\}$ is $\star$-consistent if $\Gamma_n \cup \{\neg\forall x\, \psi\}$ is.

Define $\Delta := \bigcup_n \Gamma_n$. Then, since all Γ_n are $\star$-consistent, Δ is. Moreover, Δ is *maximal* in the sense that if $\varphi \notin \Delta$ then $\Delta, \varphi \vdash \star$. From Δ's maximal

⋆-consistency it follows that if $\Delta \vdash \psi_0, \ldots, \psi_n, \star$ then $\psi_i \in \Delta$ for some ψ_i. So $T\varphi \in \Delta$ iff $\varphi \in \Delta$, since $\varphi \vdash T\varphi, \star$ and $T\varphi \vdash \varphi, \star$. In a similar way the following equivalences are seen to hold:

i. $\varphi \in \Delta$ and $\neg\varphi \in \Delta \Leftrightarrow \varphi = \# \in \Delta$ (use VIII, IX, XVIII)

ii. $\varphi \notin \Delta$ and $\neg\varphi \notin \Delta \Leftrightarrow \varphi = \star \in \Delta$ (use X, XI, XVII)

iii. $\varphi \in \Delta$ and $\neg\varphi \notin \Delta \Leftrightarrow \varphi = \top \in \Delta$ (use VII, XIII, XIX)

iv. $\varphi \notin \Delta$ and $\neg\varphi \in \Delta \Leftrightarrow \varphi = \bot \in \Delta$ (use X, XIV, XX)

As a consequence $\varphi = \psi \in \Delta$ iff it both holds that $\varphi \in \Delta \Leftrightarrow \psi \in \Delta$ and $\neg\varphi \in \Delta \Leftrightarrow \neg\psi \in \Delta$.

The maximal ⋆-consistent set of formulae Δ satisfies the following form of the *Henkin property*: (a) if $[c/x]\psi \in \Delta$ for all constants c_α then $\forall x_\alpha \psi \in \Delta$ and (b) if $\neg\forall x_\alpha \psi \in \Delta$ then $\neg[c/x]\psi \in \Delta$ for some constant c_α. To prove (a) assume that $\forall x \psi \notin \Delta$. Then $\neg T[c/x]\psi \in \Delta$ for some c, whence, since $T[c/x]\psi$ is a 2-formula, $T[c/x]\psi \notin \Delta$ and $[c/x]\psi \notin \Delta$. The proof of (b) is straightforward.

Define the relation $\approx$ between terms by $A \approx B := A = B \in \Delta$. Using the identity axioms we see that this is an equivalence relation. The equivalence class $\{B \mid A \approx B\}$ of a term A under this relation we denote with $[A]$. Note that by the Henkin property and since $\vdash \exists x\,(x = A)$, for each term A there is a constant c such that $[A] = [c]$. Now, by induction on type complexity define for each α a function Φ_α having the set of equivalence classes $\{[A] \mid A$ is of type $\alpha\}$ as its domain:

$\Phi_e([A]) = [A]$;

$\Phi_s([A]) = [A]$;

$\Phi_{\langle \alpha_1 \ldots \alpha_n \rangle}([A]) = \langle R^+, R^- \rangle$, where
$$R^+ = \{\langle \Phi_{\alpha_1}([c_1]), \ldots, \Phi_{\alpha_n}([c_n]) \rangle \mid Ac_1 \ldots c_n \in \Delta\}$$
$$R^- = \{\langle \Phi_{\alpha_1}([c_1]), \ldots, \Phi_{\alpha_n}([c_n]) \rangle \mid \neg Ac_1 \ldots c_n \in \Delta\}$$

This is well-defined; the identity axioms ensure that $\Phi_\alpha([A]) = \Phi_\alpha([A'])$ if $[A] = [A']$. To prove the converse (the injectivity of Φ_α) assume that $\Phi_{\langle \alpha_1 \ldots \alpha_n \rangle}([A]) = \Phi_{\langle \alpha_1 \ldots \alpha_n \rangle}([A'])$. Then for all suitable $c_1, \ldots, c_n$: $Ac_1 \ldots c_n \in \Delta$ iff $A'c_1 \ldots c_n \in \Delta$ and $\neg Ac_1 \ldots c_n \in \Delta$ iff $\neg A'c_1 \ldots c_n \in \Delta$. Hence $Ac_1 \ldots c_n = A'c_1 \ldots c_n \in \Delta$ for all $c_1, \ldots, c_n$. Suppose $n > 0$. By the Henkin property $\forall x_n\,(Ac_1 \ldots c_{n-1}x_n = A'c_1 \ldots c_{n-1}x_n) \in \Delta$, whence $Ac_1 \ldots c_{n-1} = A'c_1 \ldots c_{n-1} \in \Delta$ by Extensionality. Repeating this procedure as long as is necessary we find that $A = A' \in \Delta$.

We can now construct the canonical model from the equivalence classes of constants. Define D_α to be $\{\Phi_\alpha([c]) \mid c$ is a constant of type $\alpha\}$ and define $I(c) = \Phi_\alpha([c])$ for each constant c of type α. Then $M = \langle \{D_\alpha\}_\alpha, I \rangle$ is a very general model. Let a be an assignment for M such that $a(x) = \Phi_\alpha([x])$ for each variable x of type α. We prove by term induction that $\Phi_\alpha([A]) = \|A\|^{M,a}$ for each term A and so that M is a general model of Γ.

i. $\|c\|^{M,a} = I(c) = \Phi([c])$ if c is a constant;
$\|x\|^{M,a} = a(x) = \Phi([x])$ if x is a variable;

ii.

$$
\begin{aligned}
\|\neg\varphi\|^{M,a} &= -\|\varphi\|^{M,a} \\
&= \langle\{\langle\rangle \mid \neg\varphi \in \Delta\}, \{\langle\rangle \mid \varphi \in \Delta\}\rangle \\
&= \langle\{\langle\rangle \mid \neg\varphi \in \Delta\}, \{\langle\rangle \mid \neg\neg\varphi \in \Delta\}\rangle \\
&= \Phi([\neg\varphi])
\end{aligned}
$$

$$
\begin{aligned}
\|\varphi \wedge \psi\|^{M,a} &= \|\varphi\|^{M,a} \cap \|\psi\|^{M,a} \\
&= \langle\{\langle\rangle \mid \varphi \in \Delta \text{ and } \psi \in \Delta\}, \\
&\qquad \{\langle\rangle \mid \neg\varphi \in \Delta \text{ or } \neg\psi \in \Delta\}\rangle \\
&= \langle\{\langle\rangle \mid \varphi \wedge \psi \in \Delta\}, \{\langle\rangle \mid \neg(\varphi \wedge \psi) \in \Delta\}\rangle \\
&= \Phi([\varphi \wedge \psi])
\end{aligned}
$$

$$
\begin{aligned}
\|\#\|^{M,a} &= \langle 1, 1 \rangle \\
&= \langle\{\langle\rangle \mid \# \in \Delta\}, \{\langle\rangle \mid \neg\# \in \Delta\}\rangle \\
&= \Phi([\#])
\end{aligned}
$$

$$
\begin{aligned}
\|\star\|^{M,a} &= \langle 0, 0 \rangle \\
&= \langle\{\langle\rangle \mid \star \in \Delta\}, \{\langle\rangle \mid \neg\star \in \Delta\}\rangle \\
&= \Phi([\star]).
\end{aligned}
$$

iii. Since all elements of any D_α can be written as $I(c)$ for some constant c of type α, we have

$$
\begin{aligned}
\|\forall x_\alpha \varphi\|^{M,a} &= \bigcap_{d \in D_\alpha} \|\varphi\|^{M,a[d/x]} \\
&= \bigcap_{c_\alpha} \|\varphi\|^{M,a[I(c)/x]} \\
&= \bigcap_{c_\alpha} \|[c/x]\varphi\|^{M,a} \\
&= \bigcap_{c_\alpha} \Phi([[c/x]\varphi]) \\
&= \langle \bigcap_{c_\alpha}\{\langle\rangle \mid [c/x]\varphi \in \Delta\}, \\
&\qquad \bigcup_{c_\alpha}\{\langle\rangle \mid [c/x]\neg\varphi \in \Delta\}\rangle \\
&\overset{*}{=} \langle\{\langle\rangle \mid \forall x_\alpha\,\varphi \in \Delta\}, \{\langle\rangle \mid \neg\forall x_\alpha\,\varphi \in \Delta\}\rangle \\
&= \Phi([\forall x_\alpha\,\varphi]).
\end{aligned}
$$

(The identity marked * uses the Henkin property.)

iv. $\|AB\| = F^1_{\|A\|}(\|B\|) = F^1_{\Phi([A])}(\Phi([B])) = \langle R^+, R^- \rangle$, where

$$
R^+ = \{\langle d_1, \ldots, d_n \rangle \mid \langle \Phi([B]), d_1, \ldots, d_n \rangle \in \Phi([A])^+\}
$$

$$R^- = \{\langle d_1, \ldots, d_n \rangle \mid \langle \Phi([B]), d_1, \ldots, d_n \rangle \in \Phi([A])^- \}.$$

We see that

$$R^+ = \{\langle \Phi([c_1]), \ldots, \Phi([c_n]) \rangle \mid ABc_1 \ldots c_n \in \Delta\}$$
$$R^- = \{\langle \Phi([c_1]), \ldots, \Phi([c_n]) \rangle \mid \neg ABc_1 \ldots c_n \in \Delta\}$$

and so that $\|AB\| = \Phi([AB])$.

v. $\|\lambda x_\beta A\|^{M,a} =$

the R such that for all $d \in D_\beta$: $F_R^1(d) = \|A\|^{M,a[d/x]} =$

the R such that for all c_β: $F_R^1(I(c))$

$$= \|A\|^{M,a[I(c)/x]}$$
$$= \|[c/x]A\|^{M,a}$$
$$= \Phi([[c/x]A]).$$

Hence $\|\lambda x_\beta A\|^{M,a} = \langle R^+, R^- \rangle$, where:

$$R^+ = \{\langle \Phi([c]), \Phi([c_1]), \ldots, \Phi([c_n]) \rangle \mid [c/x](A)c_1 \ldots c_n \in \Delta\}$$
$$R^- = \{\langle \Phi([c]), \Phi([c_1]), \ldots, \Phi([c_n]) \rangle \mid \neg[c/x](A)c_1 \ldots c_n \in \Delta\}.$$

By Lambda Conversion $[c/x]A = \lambda x_\beta (A)c \in \Delta$ and so:

$$R^+ = \{\langle \Phi([c]), \Phi([c_1]), \ldots, \Phi([c_n]) \rangle \mid \lambda x_\beta (A)cc_1 \ldots c_n \in \Delta\}$$
$$R^- = \{\langle \Phi([c]), \Phi([c_1]), \ldots, \Phi([c_n]) \rangle \mid \neg\lambda x_\beta (A)cc_1 \ldots c_n \in \Delta\},$$

from which it follows that $\|\lambda x_\beta A\|^{M,a} = \Phi([\lambda x_\beta A])$.

vi. Since $A = B$ is a 2-formula $\neg(A = B) \in \Delta$ iff $A = B \notin \Delta$. So

$\Phi([A = B])$
$$= \langle \{\langle \rangle \mid A = B \in \Delta\}, \{\langle \rangle \mid \neg(A = B) \in \Delta\} \rangle$$
$$= \langle \{\langle \rangle \mid [A] = [B]\}, \{\langle \rangle \mid [A] \neq [B]\} \rangle$$
$$= \langle \{\langle \rangle \mid \Phi([A]) = \Phi([B])\}, \{\langle \rangle \mid \Phi([A]) \neq \Phi([B])\} \rangle$$
$$= \langle \{\langle \rangle \mid \|A\| = \|B\|\}, \{\langle \rangle \mid \|A\| \neq \|B\|\} \rangle$$
$$= \|A = B\|.$$

□

We are now ready to prove Theorem 9. Suppose $\Pi \models \Sigma$. Then each general model of Π is a general model of some $\sigma \in \Sigma$, and so the set of sentences $\Pi \cup \{\neg T\sigma \mid \sigma \in \Sigma\}$ has no general model. By the star-consistency theorem it is seen that $\Pi, \{\neg T\sigma \mid \sigma \in \Sigma\} \vdash \star$. Hence for some finite $\Pi_0 \subseteq \Pi$ and $\Sigma_0 \subseteq \Sigma$ the sequent $\Pi_0, \{\neg T\sigma \mid \sigma \in \Sigma_0\} \Rightarrow \star$ is provable. Using Lemma 1 and XXI we find that $\Pi_0 \Rightarrow \{T\sigma \mid \sigma \in \Sigma_0\}, \star$ and $\Pi_0 \Rightarrow \Sigma_0, \star$ are provable as well.

From $\Pi \models \Sigma$ it also follows that each general model of $\{\neg\sigma \mid \sigma \in \Sigma\}$ is a general model of the negation of some $\pi \in \Pi$. By an argument analogous to the one above we find that there are finite $\Pi_1 \subseteq \Pi$ and $\Sigma_1 \subseteq \Sigma$ such that $\{\neg\sigma \mid \sigma \in \Sigma_1\} \Rightarrow \{\neg\pi \mid \pi \in \Pi_1\}, \star$ is a provable sequent and hence that $\Pi_1, \star \Rightarrow \Sigma_1$ is. Now use the Cut Rule to see that $\Pi_0, \Pi_1 \Rightarrow \Sigma_0, \Sigma_1$ is provable, whence $\Pi \vdash \Sigma$. $\qquad\square$

Proof of Theorem 11

Theorem 11. ($\leq$-Persistency Theorem) *If ϑ is an analysis tree of category S, then its translation ϑ° $\leq$-persists:*

$$\text{AX9} \models \forall ij\,(i \leq j \rightarrow (\vartheta^\circ i \sqsubseteq \vartheta^\circ j)).$$

Proof. I'll give a sketch of the proof, leaving details to the reader. For each term A such that in A's type every right bracket is immediately preceded by an s define a formula $\mathsf{QP}^{\leq}(A, i, j)$, saying that A *quasi $\leq$-persists* from i to j, by the following induction:

    i. $\mathsf{QP}^{\leq}(A, i, j) = \top$, if A is of type e or type s;

    ii. $\mathsf{QP}^{\leq}(A, i, j) =$

$$\forall x_{\alpha_1} \ldots \forall x_{\alpha_n} ((\mathsf{QP}^{\leq}(x_{\alpha_1}, i, j) \wedge \ldots \wedge \mathsf{QP}^{\leq}(x_{\alpha_n}, i, j)) \rightarrow$$
$$(A x_{\alpha_1} \ldots x_{\alpha_n} i \sqsubseteq A x_{\alpha_1} \ldots x_{\alpha_n} j)),$$

    if A is of type $\langle \alpha_1 \ldots \alpha_n s \rangle$.

By an easy but long induction on the complexity of analysis trees we can prove that $\text{AX9} \models \forall ij\,(i \leq j \rightarrow \mathsf{QP}^{\leq}(\vartheta^\circ, i, j))$ for every analysis tree ϑ. From this the theorem follows immediately. $\qquad\square$

Proof of Theorem 12

Theorem 12. ($\subseteq$-Persistency Theorem) *If ϑ is an analysis tree of category S that does not contain every, a or the and if δ_1, ..., δ_n are the free variables and constants of type e occurring in ϑ° then ϑ° $\subseteq$-persists:*

$$\text{AX} \models \forall ij\,(i \subseteq j \wedge E\delta_1 i \wedge \ldots \wedge E\delta_n i \rightarrow (\vartheta^\circ i = \vartheta^\circ j)).$$

Proof. Again we'll confine ourselves to a sketch of the proof. For each term A such that in A's type every right bracket is immediately preceded by an s now define the formula $\mathsf{QP}^{\subseteq}(A, i, j)$ (A *quasi $\subseteq$-persists* from i to j) by the following induction:

    i. $\mathsf{QP}^{\subseteq}(A, i, j) = EAi$, if A is of type e;
       $\mathsf{QP}^{\subseteq}(A, i, j) = \top$, if A is of type s;

    ii. $\mathsf{QP}^{\subseteq}(A, i, j) =$

$$\forall x_{\alpha_1} \ldots \forall x_{\alpha_n} ((\mathsf{QP}^{\subseteq}(x_{\alpha_1}, i, j) \wedge \ldots \wedge \mathsf{QP}^{\subseteq}(x_{\alpha_n}, i, j)) \rightarrow$$
$$(A x_{\alpha_1} \ldots x_{\alpha_n} i = A x_{\alpha_1} \ldots x_{\alpha_n} j)),$$

    if A is of type $\langle \alpha_1 \ldots \alpha_n s \rangle$.

A tedious but straightforward induction on the complexity of analysis trees will show that if ϑ is an analysis tree of any category not containing every, a or the, and if $\delta_1, \ldots, \delta_n$ are the free variables and constants of type e occurring in ϑ° then:

$$\text{AX} \models \forall ij \, (i \subseteq j \wedge E\delta_1 i \wedge \ldots \wedge E\delta_n i \rightarrow \text{QP}^{\subseteq}(\vartheta^\circ, i, j)).$$

From this the theorem follows immediately. $\qquad\square$

Bibliography

Alves, E.H., and J.A.D. Guerzoni. 1990. Extending Montague's System: A Three Valued Intensional Logic. *Studia Logica* 49:127–132.

Anderson, A.R., and N.D. Jr. Belnap. 1975. *Entailment: the Logic of Relevance and Necessity, Vol I*. Princeton: Princeton University Press.

Andrews, P.B. 1986. *An Introduction to Mathematical Logic and Type Theory: to Truth Through Proof*. Orlando: Academic Press.

Asher, N., and D. Bonevac. 1985. How Extensional is Extensional Perception? *Linguistics and Philosophy* 8:203–228.

Asher, N., and D. Bonevac. 1987. Determiners and resource situations. *Linguistics and Philosophy* 10:567–596.

Barwise, J. 1974. Axioms for Abstract Model Theory. *Annals of Mathematical Logic* 7:221–265.

Barwise, J. 1981. Scenes and Other Situations. *Journal of Philosophy* 78:369–397. reprinted in Barwise 1989.

Barwise, J. 1989. *The Situation in Logic*. Stanford, CA: CSLI.

Barwise, J., and R. Cooper. 1981. Generalized Quantifiers and Natural Language. *Linguistics and Philosophy* 4:159–219.

Barwise, J., and J. Perry. 1983. *Situations and Attitudes*. Cambridge, Massachusetts: MIT Press.

Barwise, J., and J. Perry. 1985. Shifting Situations and Shaken Attitudes. *Linguistics and Philosophy* 8:103–161.

Belnap, N.D. Jr. 1977. A Useful Four-Valued Logic. In *Modern Uses of Multiple-Valued Logic*, ed. J.M. Dunn and G. Epstein. 8–37. Dordrecht: Reidel.

Bennett, M. 1974. *Some Extensions of a Montague Fragment of English*. Doctoral dissertation, UCLA.

van Benthem, J.F.A.K., and K. Doets. 1983. Higher-Order Logic. In *Handbook of Philosophical Logic*, ed. D.M. Gabbay and F. Guenthner. 275–329. Dordrecht: Reidel.

Bittner, M. 1994. Cross-Linguistic Semantics. *Linguistics and Philosophy* 17:53–108.

Blamey, S. 1986. Partial Logic. In *Handbook of Philosophical Logic*, ed. D.M. Gabbay and F. Guenthner. 1–70. Dordrecht: Reidel.

Carnap, R. 1929. *Abriß der Logistik.* Vienna: Verlag von Julius Springer.

Chierchia, G., and S. McConnell-Ginet. 1991. *Meaning and Grammar.* Cambridge, Massachusetts: MIT Press.

Church, A. 1940. A Formulation of the Simple Theory of Types. *Journal of Symbolic Logic* 5:56–68.

Curry, H.B. 1963. Some Logical Aspects of Grammatical Structure. In *Structure of Language and its Mathematical Aspects: Proceedings of the Twelfth Symposium in Applied Mathematics.* 56–68. AMS.

Dowty, D.R. 1982. Grammatical Relations and Montague Grammar. In *The Nature of Syntactic Representation,* ed. P. Jacobson and G.K. Pullum. 79–130. Dordrecht: Reidel.

Dowty, D.R., R.E. Wall, and S. Peters. 1981. *Introduction to Montague Semantics.* Dordrecht: Reidel.

Dunn, J.M. 1976. Intuitive Semantics for First-Degree Entailments and 'Coupled Trees'. *Philosophical Studies* 29:149–168.

Feferman, S. 1984. Toward Useful Type Free Theories I. *Journal of Symbolic Logic* 49:75–111.

Frege, G. 1892. Über Sinn und Bedeutung. In *Funktion, Begriff, Bedeutung. Fünf Logische Studien,* ed. G. Patzig. Göttingen: Vanden Hoeck.

Friedman, J., and D. Warren. 1980. Lambda Normal Forms in an Intensional Logic for English. *Studia Logica* 39:311–324.

Gabbay, D., and F. Guenthner (ed.). 1983. *Handbook of Philosophical Logic.* Dordrecht: Reidel.

Gallin, D. 1975. *Intensional and Higher-Order Modal Logic.* Amsterdam: North-Holland.

Gamut, L.T.F. 1991. *Logic, Language and Meaning.* Chicago: University of Chicago Press.

Gazdar, G. 1980. A Cross-Categorial Semantics for Coordination. *Linguistics and Philosophy* 3:407–409.

Gilmore, P.C. 1974. The Consistency of Partial Set Theory without Extensionality. In *Axiomatic Set Theory. Proceedings of Symposia in Pure Mathematics 13, Part II.* Providence. AMS.

Goldblatt, R. 1987. *Logics of Time and Computation.* Stanford: CSLI Lecture Notes.

Groenendijk, J., and M. Stokhof. 1984. *Studies on the Semantics of Questions and the Pragmatics of Answers.* Doctoral dissertation, University of Amsterdam.

Hendriks, H.L.W.H. 1993. *Studied Flexibility: Categories and Types in Syntax and Semantics.* Doctoral dissertation, University of Amsterdam.

Henkin, L. 1950. Completeness in the Theory of Types. *Journal of Symbolic Logic* 15:81–91.

Henkin, L. 1963. A Theory of Propositional Types. *Fundamenta Mathematicae* 52:323–344.

Higginbotham, J. 1983. The Logic of Perceptual Reports: an Extensional Alternative to Situation Semantics. *Journal of Philosophy* 80:100–127.

Humberstone, I.L. 1981. From Worlds to Possibilities. *Journal of Philosophical Logic* 10:313–339.

Janssen, T. 1983. *Foundations and Applications of Montague Grammar.* Doctoral dissertation, University of Amsterdam.

Janssen, T. 1984. Individual Concepts are Useful. In *Varieties of of Formal Semantics*, ed. F. Landman and F. Veltman. 171–192. Dordrecht: Foris.

Jaspars, J.O.M. 1994. *Calculi for Constructive Communication.* Doctoral dissertation, ITK, KUB. ITK Dissertation Series 1994-1/ILLC-Dissertation series 1994-4.

Kamp, H. 1983. A Scenic Tour through the Land of Naked Infinitives. Unpublished manuscript.

Keenan, E., and L. Faltz. 1978. Logical Types for Natural Language. UCLA Occasional Papers in Linguistics, 3.

Kripke, S. 1971. Identity and Necessity. In *Identity and Individuation*, ed. M. Munitz. 135–164. New York University Press.

Kripke, S. 1972. Naming and Necessity. In *Semantics of Natural Language*, ed. D. Davidson and G. Harman. 253–355. Dordrecht: Reidel.

Kripke, S. 1979. A Puzzle About Belief. In *Meaning and Use*, ed. A. Margalit. 239–283. Dordrecht: Reidel.

Lambek, J., and P.J. Scott. 1981. Intuitionist Type Theory and Foundations. *Journal of Philosophical Logic* 10:101–115.

Landman, A. 1986. *Towards a Theory of Information.* Doctoral dissertation, University of Amsterdam.

Landman, A., and F. Veltman (ed.). 1984. *Varieties of Formal Semantics.* Dordrecht: Foris.

Langholm, T. 1988. *Partiality, Truth and Persistence.* Stanford: CSLI Lecture Notes.

Lapierre, S. 1992. A Functional Partial Semantics for Intensional Logic. *Notre Dame Journal of Formal Logic* 33:517–541.

Lepage, F. 1992. Partial Functions in Type Theory. *Notre Dame Journal of Formal Logic* 33:493–516.

Lewis, D. 1974. 'Tensions. In *Semantics and Philosophy*, ed. M.K. Munitz and P.K. Unger. New York: New York University Press.

Mates, B. 1952. Synonymity. In *Semantics and the Philosophy of Language*, ed. Linsky. 111–136. Urbana: The University of Illinois Press.

Montague, R. 1970. Universal Grammar. In *Montague 1974.* 222–246.

Montague, R. 1973. The Proper Treatment of Quantification in Ordinary English. In *Montague 1974.* 247–270.

Montague, R. 1974. *Formal Philosophy.* New Haven: Yale University Press.

Muskens, R.A. 1989a. Going Partial in Montague Grammar. In *Semantics and Contextual Expression. Proceedings of the Sixth Amsterdam Colloquium*, ed. R. Bartsch, J.F.A.K. van Benthem, and P. van Emde Boas. Dordrecht: Foris.

Muskens, R.A. 1989b. A Relational Formulation of the Theory of Types. *Linguistics and Philosophy* 12:325–346.

Muskens, R.A. 1991a. Anaphora and the Logic of Change. In *Logics in AI, Proceedings of JELIA '90*, ed. J. Van Eijck. Berlin: Springer-Verlag.

Muskens, R.A. 1991b. Hyperfine-grained Meanings in Classical Logic. *Logique et Analyse* 133/134:159–176.

Muskens, R.A. 1995a. Combing Montague Semantics and Discourse Representation. *Linguistics and Philosophy*.

Muskens, R.A. 1995b. Tense and the Logic of Change. In *Lexical Knowledge in the Organization of Language*, ed. U. Egli, E.P. Pause, C. Schwarze, A. Von Stechow, and G. Wienold. 147–183. Amsterdam: John Benjamins.

Orey, S. 1959. Model Theory for the Higher Order Predicate Calculus. *Transactions of the American Mathematical Society* 92:72–84.

Perry, J. 1984. Contradictory Situations. In *Landman and Veltman 1984*. 313–323.

Perry, J. 1986. From Worlds to Situations. *Journal of Philosophical Logic* 15:83–107.

Putnam, H. 1954. Synonymity and the Analysis of Belief Sentences. *Analysis* 14:114–122.

Quine, W.V.O. 1953. *From a Logical Point of View*. New York: Harper and Row.

Russell, B. 1908. Mathematical Logic as Based on the Theory of Types. *American Journal of Mathematics* 30:222–262.

Schönfinkel, M. 1924. Über die Bausteine der mathematischen Logik. *Mathematische Annalen* 92:305–316.

Searle, J.R. 1958. Proper Names. *Mind* 67:166–173.

Thijssse, E.G.C. 1992. *Partial Logic and Knowledge Representation*. Doctoral dissertation, Eburon, Delft; ITK/KUB, Tilburg.

Tichy, P. 1982. Foundations of Partial Type Theory. *Reports on Mathematical Logic* 14:59–72.

Veltman, F. 1985. *Logics for Conditionals*. Doctoral dissertation, University of Amsterdam.

Visser, A. 1984. Four Valued Semantics and the Liar. *Journal of Philosophical Logic* 13:181–212.

Von Stechow, A. 1974. ϵ-λ kontextfreie Sprachen: Ein Beitrag zu einer natürlichen formalen Semantik. *Linguistische Berichte* 34:1–33.

Woodruff, P.W. 1984. Paradox, Truth and Logic, Part I: Paradox and Truth. *Journal of Philosophical Logic* 13:213–232.

Name Index

137

Subject Index